I0549490

Sharing Our Journeys 2
(Queer BIPOC Elders Tell Their Stories)

Edited by Ron Kearse
Introduction by Rebecca Mabanglo-Mayor

Filidh Publishing

Copyright 2022 Ron Kearse

All rights reserved.

Filidh Publishing, Victoria, BC.

ISBN 978-1-927848-70-8 (Soft Cover)

Cover Design by Danny Weeds
Front cover photo credits:
(Top photo) Stock photo ID: 1153753772 (FatCamera
https://fat.camera/)
(Lower photo) Stock photo ID:1201593827 (Kuplcoo)
Back cover photo credits:
Stock photo ID: 1365232011 and Stock photo ID: 1370046414
(kate_sept2004 Toronto, Canada http://instagram.com/weekendimages)

Foreward

A rare treat in the not-for-profit world is receiving a grant which will make an impact in people's lives. Rarer still is to receive funding for a project which intimately touches one's own life and experience as well. Yet that's what happened in 2017 when Alexandra Neighbourhood House – where I work as the community developer – received funding through the federal government's "Canada 150" program.

As a gay man privileged to have enjoyed the support of a vibrant community in the City of Vancouver, my experience working in the farther-flung suburban cities (specifically Surrey and White Rock) brought into stark relief the loneliness, isolation, and invisibility of sexual and gender-variant people who call these places home. The challenges to community engagement and participation are intensified in older 2SLGBTQ+ adults, many of whom find themselves back in the closet as they enter residential facilities.

As a project, "Sharing Our Journeys" was aimed at reducing the social isolation of queer and trans elders. The goal was approached in two ways. The first, "Journeying Together," was an intergenerational dinner and discussion. Participants in our Youth Space prepared a main course, supplemented by elders. Afterwards, an older adult shared their personal story, followed by a facilitated conversation. The activity was so successful, participants requested it continues after the end of the project.

"Sharing Our Journeys" was also the name given to the second project activity: a published anthology of personal memoirs from local 2SLGBTQ+ seniors. Our hope was that this would create connections between contributors, under the mentorship of editor Ron Kearse, as well as provide them the opportunity to share their stories with family and friends, deepening those connections as well. Ron was inspired by this experience to develop a second volume of the anthology, focused on the narratives of older queer/trans adults who identify as BIPOC.

Intersectional identities create multiple vulnerabilities, and so I welcome Ron's initiative in creating this second volume as a means of affirming visibility and representation of communities of colour in the 2SLGBTQ+ experience...especially in suburban and rural communities, where supports are chronically deficient.

As I write this, 2SLGBTQ+ advocates and service providers are beginning an initiative to develop a centre to serve the queer/trans population living in Surrey and its neighbouring cities – hosting a population of around 800,000 people. The success of community building begins with drawing one another into participation through connection and conversation. Let *Sharing Our Journeys 2* be an important conversation starter as we work together to co-create communities of loving inclusion.

Neil Fernyhough,
Manager Community Programs,
Alexandra Neighbourhood House

Neil Ferryhough

Neil was born, raised, and is rooted in the Coast Salish territory of British Columbia. He has a varied background working with vulnerable people; first, as a child protection worker in northern and rural communities, as a priest working in the disadvantaged urban neighbourhood of Vancouver's Downtown Eastside, and a finally as a community developer and programmer for Alex House – a place-based nonprofit organization serving the suburban communities of Surrey, White Rock, and Cloverdale, BC. The goal of Neil's work is to draw people, especially those who are marginalized or vulnerable, from isolation into connection and participation. In his free time, Neil enjoys outdoor activities, gardening, and cooking.

(photo credit: provided by author)

Introduction

Most days of the week, you can find me at my local Starbucks writing, reading, musing... the usual with a decaf grande mocha with coconut milk, no whip on the side. I'm here often enough, the usual baristas know my order and only ask the size in case I'm feeling more tall than grande. Overhead, music plays to drown the details of patron orders and the whoosh of the espresso machines.

Usually tunes by Dua Lipa, Maroon 5, Harry Styles, and such play overhead but occasionally, I'll hear a song I heard on the bus to high school – "Don't You Want Me," "The Tide is High," "Our House," – and I start humming the tune and sway in my seat. The songs always bring a smile to my face, and, until recently, I was unaware of the years the songs were released until I found them on a YouTube "80's Oldies" playlist.

Oldies?

Aren't the Oldies tunes by Frank Sinatra and the Rat Pack? Crooners like Bing Crosby? Maybe, at a stretch, Herb Alpert and the Tijuana Brass?

And if my favourite songs were "oldies," what did that make me, someone who graduated high school when Reagan was serving his first term as US president?

Time is a funny thing. I've always thought of myself as not really attached to time. I struggle to remember my age when asked because day-to-day becomes month-to-month becomes year-to-year (and it's not just the menopause talking). Moments punctuate my memory, and if I reel back to the 80s, I remember when AIDS became a crisis as secret lives were revealed, and men died at an alarming rate. In 1985 the first AIDS Memorial Quilt was displayed to honour over one thousand men who had died in San Francisco alone. In 1988, activists began to use "LGBT" to include cis men, cis women, and transgender people. In between, the Challenger launched and exploded in 1986. Sometime before 9/11, Freddie Mercury died, Diana and Charles divorced, and Google was founded.

Old news.

Advertising is unkind to 'oldies,' making claims to remove wrinkles, tighten bellies, and hide white hair with the 'perfect product.' Being old is being a 'has been,' a Gen-Xer at best, one forgotten between the Boomers and the Millennials. Many have the privilege to simply move on with their lives and hope their retirement plans will at least match the ones their parents made during the Reagan Years. The LGBTQIA+ community does not have that luxury. We have been fighting for our identity, our lives, our peace of mind since before many of the writers in this anthology were in grade school.

Awareness, activism, and community have moved us, though, from being 'old' to being 'elders' – ones who remember what was in the hope that the ones coming up behind us will know they don't have to recreate the wheel when it comes to surviving and thriving as a queer person.

CJ Jackman-Zigante reveals that her respect for elders came from her culture, people who were strict because of the deep scrutiny of others who examined every detail of a child's behaviour to judge the quality of their parents. Elders kept the stories of their history, one that didn't appear in textbooks or discussed in classrooms. Each child gained the right to their stories of survival through obedience to the rules. As persons of colour, they dealt with enough prejudice because they could not hide, so why look for another fight? Yet, she had an uncle who was unabashedly gay, and later saw the dehumanization the AIDS epidemic caused. The question "what shall I do with this power?" resonates throughout her essay, a true trait of being an elder.

In his essay, Cornel Thomas tells the tale of growing up Creole Catholic who knew from a young age about his attraction to boys and men. He also knew that his attraction wasn't in 'the norm' and was actively rejected within his community, especially when there was a significant age difference. When the FBI became involved in his case, he became keenly aware of the dangers of his identity. Like many, he kept his gay life under the radar, yet followed the example of his own elder – a cousin who was openly gay and in a long-term relationship with a white man. Year after year, he built his own courage to be who he knew himself to be, walking the tightrope of role model and authenticity within a vibrant community he was becoming increasingly involved in. He has embodied the elder trait of persistence and humility in adversity.

"If you love, love openly" goes the Zen Buddhist parable and Gloria Jackson-Nefertiti's essay centers on the intimacy and challenges of being polyamorous, a segment of the greater community that is frequently mistaken as little more than casual sex. Often, partners draw affection, intimacy, and companionship from one to several others in ways unique to each partner. At the heart of the essay is her realization that she was a secret when it came to her partner's life. What is the cost of feeling loved? Instead of staying in a relationship that did not honour her presence and essence, she learned to accept the love of others who supported her unconditionally. Elders in our community learn to keep hope in the midst of heartbreak and become trusted mentors to those yet to feel the pain and joy of loving whole-heartedly.

Jayantha Withanage didn't have elders in the LGBTQIA+ community who could guide and mentor him. In fact, he had no vocabulary for his feelings or any examples, positive or negative, of the community's experiences. In the 1950s, censorship in popular media was rampant in his home country of Sri Lanka, but a yearning to travel gave him the chance to search for the resources he needed. Leaving Sri Lanka, though, was difficult and over the course of his adulthood, he slowly created a path where he could live his life more authentically with each step. Police raids and the fear of punishment because of gay activities was a constant danger and I, as a Gen-Xer, am in awe of this Boomer's grit and nerve. Elders are fierce in ways that help me feel brave in the face of adversity.

The Transgender segment of our community is one that awes me daily because of their ferocious desire to be their authentic selves, to be the whole person they know themselves to be despite the markers imposed by the medical community and religious teachings. Oscar Hall is a survivor, one who yearned for acceptance even as those who surrounded him as a child created a deep sense of self-loathing and rejection through bullying and the ever-present belief that he had a mistaken sense of self. His desire to be loved as he is could be considered universal and yet, the cost of that love is higher than the privileged population could imagine let alone pay. His suffering is the kind that has killed numerous people and yet he remains and speaks his truth. As a mother of a transgender/nonbinary child, I look to elders like him with hope and determination to protect and defend the trans community's right to be as they are, as they know themselves to be.

Because LGBTQIA+ people are forced to 'pass' in order to survive and live mainstream culture as much as possible, we become isolated from the LGBTQIA+ culture as it grows and develops. Silence keeps us from accessing the very support we so desperately need to feel safe even as we take risks. Still, it can be difficult to connect with others in the community because of differences between regional cultures. How can we explain the intricacies of cultural expectations that have to be navigated even as we seek love and companionship in an authentic way? Shinji Kasama tells his story as the youngest child of a large Japanese family and explains how there was very little information on homosexuality in central Japan in the 1970s. As he grew up, cultural expectations to conform and came in the form of his family's pointed questions about jobs, marriage prospects, and physical distance. To disappoint our families feels unthinkable. Silence and isolation seem best for all concerned. Kasama writes about his struggle to be with the man he loves in a country where he is under less scrutiny even though it would mean leaving his family of origin. As an elder, he hopes for a better future for the Queer Community, one where members can enjoy the same rights and privileges that members of the mainstream often take for granted.

Like other authors in this anthology, Agustin Restrepo struggled with understanding his own sexual desires within the constraints of race, class, and religion. Thankfully, he felt supported by his family because of the fun and love they shared even though they were unaware of his sexuality. Restrepo himself was in denial until he read a college text about human sexuality and learned the term "Closet Queen." He recognized himself immediately and was keenly aware that being out in "Catholic macho country" would be dangerous. Moving to the US seemed the best option, but he suffered many setbacks during the worst years of the AIDS epidemic and the height of experimental drug usage. Still, he persisted, travelled the world, married, and navigated being forced to be out to his family via social media. His story shows, like the others in this anthology, that it is possible to be out while retaining a sense of self and connection to one's culture of origin.

Overhead here at Starbucks, Jon Batiste sings his song "Freedom," a song released in 2021 but speaks of what we have all sought as we grew older – the freedom to be ourselves and the right to be safe in our sexual and gender expressions. 'Old' is often associated with 'irrelevance' and old people are seen as 'out of touch.' The elders in this anthology, though, show the importance of sharing personal stories and that the isolations we suffer can be overcome with the power of persistence, hope, and even joy. We all want a better future where dignity and safety are a right for every person no matter the race, sexuality, mental health, or economic status. We elders are reaching back to the next generation hoping they know we have their backs, that we'll do everything we can to fulfill our mutual dream of freedom wherever we are, wherever we go.

Rebecca Mabanglo-Mayor
Author, Editor, Storyteller

Rebecca Mabanglo-Mayor

Rebecca Mabanglo-Mayor's non-fiction, poetry, and short fiction have appeared in print and online in several journals and anthologies including Katipunan Literary Magazine, Growing Up Filipino II: More Stories for Young Adults, Kuwento: Small Things, and Beyond Lumpia, Pansit, and Seven Manangs Wild: An Anthology. Her poetry chapbook Pause Mid-Flight was released in 2010. She is also the co-editor of True Stories: The Narrative Project Vols. I-IV, and her poetry and essays have been collected in Dancing Between Bamboo Poles. She has been performing as a storyteller since 2006 and specializes in stories based on Filipino folktales and Filipino-American history.

(photo credit: provided by author)

Table of Contents

CJ Jackman-Zigante

Canadian Actress raised in the east end of Toronto, Ontario. A child actor beginning at the age of seven, spent four years as a regular dancer on CityTV's Boogie before landing her first role in the feature film The Kidnapping Of The President, with William Shatner, Hal Holbrook and Eva Gardner. Switching direction to pursue music, she joined her uncle, Charlie Ecstein, in the family show band 'Something Kinda Different' as the lead female vocalist spending fourteen years travelling across Canada. In '91, she moved to the west coast of Canada to work in film and television once again. British Columbia opened several other artistic opportunities and led to time spent on stage, both in theatre, cabaret and stand-up comedy clubs across the lower mainland. The change also rekindled her love of writing, fully immersing her life in the arts. She has gone on to establish herself as a triple-threat entertainer adding director, producer, published author, writer, and playwright to her list of accomplishments and credits.

When not working on film or television projects, armed with her love of crafting and artistic design, she spends time creating original works under her company name, Zigante Designs Boutique. C J resides in Beautiful British Columbia, Canada's Fraser Valley, with her husband of more than twenty years and her significant other of seven years, along with their two adorable fur babies, Basil & Ginger. They are one big happy family.

(Photo credit: provided by author)

Black Queer Elder

If you were to ask me what an elder was, I would say it was someone who, as a child, we were taught to respect simply because they were older, (even if some we knew were not necessarily wiser). Respect your elders meant saying yes sir and yes ma'am to any adult you came into contact with, whether family or stranger. This rule came with punishment for disobeying and disrespecting that. Which in my day could be meted out by whomever you showed disrespect while also having the bonus of being dragged home to report your bad behaviour to your parents, who would then (well mine anyway), add to your punishment for good measure!

As a child, I took great pride in hearing people tell my mother how polite and well-behaved I was, which also saved me an ass-whupping in the process. I knew too, it made my mother stand just a little taller. I would come to understand later that her need to look strict in the public eye, (read to white folks), had to do with the unfair reflection on her not just as a mother, but as a woman of colour, based on her children's behaviour. It was that same magnifying glass that fueled her strict adherence to education, ensuring that well before entering kindergarten, not only was I made to know my address and phone number off by heart, but also how to read and write at what was then considered grade three level. Black kids heard time and time again how we had to be twice as smart, twice as good as any white kid, because the world kept trying to paint us as shiftless and lazy, with very low learning potential...

So, if you were to ask me what a black elder was, I would say they were the keepers of our stories the ones who taught us where we came from in order to get where we are. The ones who battled the indignities of slavery and Jim Crow, marching in protest for the right to live where we chose, marry whomever we loved, no matter the race or colour, and the right to vote for those freedoms.

A black elder would have been my great grandmother who helped tend the sick and my grandfather who was one of the first police constables in Annapolis Valley, in Nova Scotia. Those and so many whose life adventures my mother would recount at gatherings, and every other family member of an age, shared stories of their journeys, because 'they' walked through the fires and were here to damn well tell us children about it! My mother's strictness, when it came to making sure that I earned the right to claim those stories, often left me feeling that pressure was unfair and unjust.

Right up until that day, when I was in grade seven, and the teacher told me not to worry about trying to understand what was written on the board, and just to copy it down. In his words, "You people are like monkeys, you just mimic anyway." So, while we may have grudgingly for a time accepted separate but equal, the path to a new day was being paved.

Which leads me to yet another if...

If you were then to ask me, what a black queer elder was, I might not have known the answer right away. Of course, it's a given that it would encompass all that each description and especially that of a black elder held, but would there not be so much more? As a person of colour you can never hide that from the world it is the first and sometimes only thing that anyone sees when you step out your front door. It enters every single space before you step a foot in it. Seen through windows, side-eyed on buses and passing strangers in the street. But as a black gay person, which at one time meant becoming an expert at hiding that away, not just from others, but also denying it even to themselves. Because it was hard enough as a person of colour, who needed or wanted another battle to fight? Even today there are stories with heartbreaking endings, the suicide rate is near epidemic and as we have seen, there are still places where being gay can just as easily get you killed as being black. How far have we really come? I can say now, however far we've come that as I look back I'm so grateful, for having had Black and Queer elders in my life to mould and shape who I feel I've become.

So, what magic did they weave, what ancient ancestral wisdom, did they pass down to me, in some sacred ceremonial circle to prepare me to go out into the world? Was there some finite moment where all was revealed and the mantle passed? In pondering this monumental question, came the discovery that while this title comes with lofty expectations, it is apparently quite possible to become one without ever realizing you are, or even knowing just what it was you'd done to be made one. Perhaps it is as simple as someone, in this instance me, taking the opportunity to speak of them with reverence. Because for me to find myself here being considered, a black queer elder, it would be impossible to embrace the honour without first giving them their due.

~ In Honor of The Elders ~

How can I honour you my forefathers and mothers, my ancestors, sisters and brothers? How can I show you the reverence you deserve, for the battles you waged, so that someday I may have the right to set these words on paper or page in this the cyber age? How can I convey to you the deep gratitude that lives within my heart yet share the sadness and the pain that you endured?

How can I honour you, when words seem so small in comparison to your sacrifice?

Tell your story, I hear you say. Show the world that we existed, that we lived and our story should never be forgotten.

Leave out no detail for each one was a promise of a better day.

Leave out no moment of joy, for those gave us strength to fight and live on when all that we loved,

had been taken from us like breath on the wind, gone.

Leave no moment of victory untold for each one was the gateway to freedom,

if not for us, then for our children and our children's children,

for you, who sits here writing these words, and you,

who sits here reading them.......

In that way, you honour and lift us up.

[© 2009 / 2019, 2021 C J Jackman Zigante]

When I was a kid, family gatherings were common and in mine, it seemed that we were always at someone's house for a cookout or holiday get-together. While it seemed, we gathered at just about everyone's home including ours from time to time, house party central seemed to be at my aunt Georgina's (Georgie for short) house

Each party was always jam-packed, the Johnson clan was huge and the list of families related by blood or marriage was big enough to lay claim to several small towns in Nova Scotia (the joke was that you couldn't walk two feet without running into a relative, which is why they all moved to Toronto so they could find someone to marry).

With a house this full, good food was plenty, laughter and cheer were always in the air, and come evening there would be drinking and dancing, (ok that started when everyone got there), but really took flight around 8ish. Then inevitably before us young'uns were relegated to the basement while grown folks talked about old times, we kids were rounded up for the traditional house party staple the Motown get down. That's where the entertainment bug first hit me.

I found myself performing (or rather lip-syncing), songs like: Ain't no Way, Respect, Our Day Will Come and Stop in the Name of Love, to name but a few. I wasn't exempt from the odd Tammy Tyrell Marvin Gaye duets either. My cousin Bucky looked so much like Smokey Robinson that he could have passed for his love child so of course he covered all of Smokey's grooves, and my brother who couldn't dance if his life depended on it, (don't tell him because at nearly 65 he still thinks he can).

My cousin William who was called that because Bill Bing my grandfather's and great grandfather's name, was very popular in our family and three of my cousins and my brother were all named after him, so in order to determine who was being hollered for, they found creative ways to let them know who was who Bill, Billy, [my brother], BJ, and William, covered the Temptations, Spinners, Dramatics, then backed up cousin Bucky as the Miracles.

Meanwhile, my cousins Heart, Hope, Robin and I held the girl groups down. Of course, I was the biggest ham so I bet you can guess who played Diana Ross. Now while the Motown get down was usually left to us kids to perform, once in a while, when the spirit moved him there was my Uncle Lester, cousin Lester really, but because he was an elder it was decided that he be addressed as such, by us kids.

Uncle Lester whose finely pressed hair held no kinks and looked like James Brown had styled it himself. It never dawned on me that he was gay, until I was in my teens, back then I thought he was just flashy, an oh so cool. His performances usually marked the end of our Motown review. So just before we were sent off, he would take my hand and say come on girl, you know what we got to do and while someone would slip a record on the player we took our spot and posed and in perfect, rhythmic harmony, we would do our dance moves, holding brushes for mics and gave them what they came for...

We never knew what song/s they were going to pick for us and we had to get the singers' personalities just right so you know our improv game was tight. We rose to the challenge each and every time, including encores. And as the last note faded and we took our bows to the applause, he would lower his hand to me, for a give me five on the black hand side. Being around him was always electric and I found ways to avoid that basement so I could sit and listen to him tell stories. He was loud, funny and even I knew he was saying outrageous things and probably dirty double entendre things too....

I knew he had gone blue when suddenly my presence was noticed, (sitting quietly seen and unheard had its privileges). That is, until grown folk talk went places children shouldn't go, and I reluctantly, and as slowly as possible, did as I was told. Beyond a shadow of a doubt Uncle/ Cousin Lester, would count as #1 amongst my black queer elders.

We never really talked about it, but I think he knew I was queer before I did. Who knows maybe that "gaydar" thing, is real! All I know is that he doted on me more than any of my cousins. My cousin Lester, who refused to dial down his feminine side and made velvet leisure pant suits, turtle necks 'n' Beatle boots look so funky fresh n cool, that I damned near lost my mind when he gave me my very own black velvet jacket to wear, with my mod knit turtle neck sweater, green plaid miniskirt n black penny loafers. And yes, honey my beehive hair with headband setting it all off perfectly, were on point.

I look back now in awe and reverence since all of this living out loud was occurring in a time when we were still far from accepted as people of colour, let alone gay. Uncle Lester was not afraid to catch a beating or give one to stand up for himself and call someone out on their ignorance. He taught me, by example, how to do the same without flinching. He probably never even knew it, or maybe he did, but it just never needed clarifying between us. He was bold in your face and unapologetic, I'm pretty sure that's where I got my attitude from. He lived openly with and finally married, his life partner, David, after over 40 years of being together, when it became legal in 2003. After a brief battle with cancer in 2018, he passed away.

Thank you, Uncle Lester for helping me find my shine and learn how to stand in my power! I think of you every time I play some Motown.

Where Uncle Lester was ready to throw down physically for his right to be who he was, Uncle Raul was more cerebral and understated in his approach. He wasn't in the closet he was just more conservative, or, he would say, polished in his efforts. Uncle Raul lived his life as openly as legally possible, unashamed of who he was, he set about working hard at building a business and sterling reputation in publishing, together with his life partner and letting his hair down or lack thereof on weekends. He taught me, how not to be ashamed of who I loved and to stand tall in my blackness all at the same time. His personal life details for the world at large, were nobody's business, though he never hid it from family friends or close colleagues.

He just wasn't marching in protest or fighting in bars or on the streets. He fought with his pocketbook, buying a home in an upper-middle-class area of Don Mills, on a street that most likely saw them being the only black folks, (or if not, then amongst very few). I know on our street we were the only black family until 1972.

Uncle Raul wore a suit and tie pretty much everywhere he went, the only exceptions, family gatherings, summer barbeques and at his own home, whenever he was the one throwing the party. But even then, he was a sharp-dressing man. His taste ran to turtle necks and tailored leisure pants; I'm willing to bet there was a jacket to match hanging in his closet. When I think of his house, I realize my love of interior design and decorating came from him too.

Once I was living on my own, I was obsessed with antique phones. He'd had several in his house. From the elegant art deco princess phones, to the early Victorian phone that had no dial, you just cranked an arm on the side and asked for the operator to connect you. He had a black phone in his office that reminded me of the phone that sat on Humphrey Bogart's desk in the Maltese

Falcon. And oh, don't get me started about his paintings, modern works of abstract art, colourful, bold, impeccably framed.

His furniture was mid-century teak oh, what I wouldn't give to have inherited every stick of that furniture especially the side table and dining room set. I love the style sleekness and form of the era. Clearly with such impeccable taste and style I should have known. How could they all have taught me so much without ever knowing that they had about life love queerness? I wish I could tell them that most of all, they taught me that gayness was just like anything else in life, open to our own distinct personal interpretation. How we choose to represent ourselves and be seen by the world, from the rebel in blue jeans to suit tie button-down shirt with high heel pumps!

Thank you, Uncle Raul.

My wake-up call happened in my twenties. By then, on my own and a single mother, I watched the world's reaction to, and treatment of those afflicted by the AIDS epidemic. So many were losing loved ones.

That's when I began to see just how much of a battle to be accepted as human and queer was being fought. I began to see the ugly side, hear the words of hate see the violence and insensitivity to the plight of the LGBTQ community, and wondered how I had missed all of that before. The rebel in me finally stepped up and instead of just living my life, I started 'living' my life, out loud and very proud though truth be told I was never really in the closet, because by example I had seen that life could be lived for the most part, on my terms. But I wanted more I wanted to be visible, heard not just seen. I kept thinking to myself, what could I do to get even louder? Pride answered my prayers. Less than two years after moving to BC, I marched in my very first parade, dressed as Magda Ledgerdomaine from the play, *Vampire Lesbians of Sodom*, and I remembered thinking, I'd finally earned my place. That night, my mother called to let me know folks back in Ontario had seen me marching and called her in shock! All she said was, "did ya' have to have one tit hanging out?" Why, yes mom. Yes, I did.

Which brings me full circle back to here and now. You would think by all that's written here and the extent of how deeply I've said my uncles Lester and Raul's presence impacted me, that they were a part of my everyday life but, the reality is the memories I'm sharing, all stem from those house gatherings, just fleeting remnants of time, (and those I must reiterate, from the viewpoint of a child at that). I wish there were more I could share of those days but just like that one day, there were no more house parties. Some I guess I missed because, well life happened, I grew up, time moved on, I boarded a plane and headed out west. The last time I saw my uncles and far too many other members of my family, was at my son's funeral in 1995. A story for another time perhaps.

So then, with the pedigree I stem from, am I truly a black queer elder? Being the eternal youth that I am, the thought had never really crossed my mind. But now, having reached this pinnacle-of-pinnacled junctures in time, I'm inclined to believe that yes, yes, I am a black queer elder. There was no grand ceremony, no public announcement in the news, not even a big house party with booze and a cake! But now having accepted the mantle, what shall I do with this power?

I mean, do I now have some obligation to impart the wisdom I have gained in life, to those up n 'coming out' gifted young black queer kids? What could I possibly tell them that would matter?

Today's kids are raising their fists and daring to be as authentically themselves as they can be, whether the world is ready for them to be so, or not! If maybe I had one small, wee, pet peeve it would be, maybe it's just me, but hear me out. Lately, it seems everyone is so much more focused, on fighting over being called by the proper pronouns, that it seems they've forgotten we are still fighting to be allowed, to just be who we are, whether others know what to call us or not! Reading that back to myself, I kind of feel like I have to add, 'Hey kids, get off my lawn!' but I have to be honest...

See I'm not saying identity isn't important, it matters! Lesbian, Gay, Bisexual, Transgender, Queer and/or Questioning, Intersex, Asexual, Two-Spirit, and the countless affirmative ways in which people self-identify are important. I admit where I find myself 100% on board with that and raising my voice, just as high, is for the transgender community. I am fully in support of being recognized and addressed for who you are and who you love. I just feel there is where, the situation warrants it far more importantly, than whether someone gets 'my' personal pronouns right. I am in the right body and even though, I identify as gender-fluid, I don't care enough, whether you call me him, her, or they. But then that being said, the odds of my being 'dead named' are pretty slim.

Yes, it should all be important to how you see yourself and how you feel and find yourself, so that when you stand up and demand to be seen as you know you are meant to be, you will stand in absolute conviction. They can never take that away from you, even with ignorance or hate. So, scratch that, maybe I'm just being crotchety and maybe, all I really have to do, is just enjoy the title and perks that come with it. I hear they let the Elders ride the Pride floats instead of walking during the parade...I'll take it!

Postscript:

With the passing of my Aunt Leona, followed by my mother in 2019, all the elders of my childhood are now gone. May they rest in remembrance and peace.

Cornell Thomas

Cornell Thomas is presently in his company's pre-retirement structure, soon-to-be fully retired with 40 years of service. He is living in the cities of Lake Charles, Louisiana and Billings, Montana, at any given time, where the newlyweds (one year as of Feb 2021) have their homes. Cornell has an A.G.S. (Associate of General Studies) and B.S. (Bachelor of Science) degree in General Studies with a major in Behavioral Science and a double-minor in Psychology and English.

(Photo credit: provided by author)

Cornel Thomas' Story

My story goes – born out of wedlock to a single mother in Lake Charles, Louisiana. The year was 1965. I was the first of four children, three boys and one girl. My maternal grandparents and my (Aunt) mother's only sister would be major influences throughout my youth and life. Our family are Creole of Color, multiracial. We grew up in the Catholic faith. This was not the usual Catholic Mass, being in a community of colour. Oh, we prayed like Roman Catholics but sang like Southern Baptists, and I loved to sing. I owe a lot to my humble upbringing in the South. That laid the groundwork for who I am today.

When I was eight going on nine, my mother, now married, moved us cross country to the Watts district of Los Angeles, California where my stepfather went for a job. I acclimated easily enough. Children truly are resilient creatures. That time in my life would be what is today called a life event (i.e., experiences that disrupt one's life bringing a substantial change), this would be when everything changed. Now, to be clear, I knew I liked boys/men already. As a first-born child, I was more mature than many of my contemporaries. I understood that same-sex attractions were not 'the norm' growing up during the 1970s. It was frowned upon even more as a person of colour. My grandmother, in her wisdom, used to tell us, "we all have our cross to bear." This felt like it was mine. It was my secret growing up. As a child, I had a few sexual experimental moments with other boys before the move, but California brought things to another level.

During my youth I was very shy, and introverted, some called it 'momma's boy.' I was close to my mother, my grandmother, and my aunt (who was like my third mom). Maybe that is why, looking back, I attracted the attention of two adult men in Los Angeles. Both engaged in sex with me. One was 18 and the other 25. As a child, devoid of a father figure most of my life, and not close to my stepdad, I can see today how any attention from men back then was welcomed. Having reconciled myself to my homosexuality early in life, I did not feel the weight of negative energy from these physical situations. To me it was a form of affection. I do not think that I ever questioned it. It was not until the oldest man's indiscretions with me were discovered and revealed, (by my slightly older step-cousin who spent the night one evening and confronted him, aggressively), that my parents got law enforcement involved. This next part is all a bit of a blur to me, the time at the FBI's office. I am sure I was shielded from much of the fallout. He had, after all, been our babysitter and next-door neighbour. The thing that most stood out in my memory was being made to reveal to mom I had been molested (what the adults called it.) My step-cousin blurted out "the babysitter is messing with you" in the car as we were in the driveway, heading off to Disneyland. My stepdad stopped the car and made me go tell my mother (who was not going with us). That walk from the car, up the stairs, and into the apartment felt like death row on the way to an execution, mine. I still see her standing in the bathroom, brushing her teeth, how she slapped me as the words spilt from my lips about what was happening right under her roof. She began to cry.

I do not know whatever finally happened with the charges. In my memory time moved quickly to the end of school.

My brothers and I flew on a plane for the first time in 1975, heading to our grandparent's home down South. The novelty of that was we were unchaperoned. Three small children on a plane without an adult was not a thing one could do today. Somehow, mom talked the airlines into that. I remember feeling, being the oldest, I had to look out for my younger brothers. That feeling would remain with me into adulthood. The airline stewardess was kind and checked on us as her duties allowed. I remember holding my brother's hands walking through the airport terminal upon exiting the plane in Houston, Texas. Looking for any recognition on the faces of adults we passed, knowing somewhere our family was waiting there to receive us. My uncle (mother's only brother) ferried us to the car where my grandmother was waiting. I remember asking if she was not happy to see us (something about an expression I picked up on but the truth behind that moment was yet to be revealed). She simply said she was tired. My grandparent's house was always the place I most felt at home. It and they gave me stability and a foundation. My life back in California mostly faded into the background. My mother and I had made a deal before I left Los Angeles. I would not be going back. My maternal grandparents would raise me. It would be that very summer of 1975 my mother would die. Unbeknownst to me, she had a heart disease. She had shared this news with her mother and father at some point, but her children had no idea. We never saw her again. My world crashed around me.

The love of my family kept us together. Time helped me move forward but it would be many years before I learned to move on. I just did not have the tools to do it through my youth, and early adult life. There was always a weight I carried, my mother's death, my absent father, my realization of being homosexual, worry about what would happen to us if my grandparents died. Heavy topics for a child to have to hold, but somehow, they did not break me. They only held me down with fear. That fear kept me from spreading my wings and flying. The one constant family member I saw who was openly gay, widely loved and accepted was my older cousin from Beaumont, Texas. He and his white lover came often to my grandmother's home. Our house was ground zero where family and friends flocked to when in the city. Some came for my grandmother's wise advice and most all for the good creole cooking. The stove was usually covered in pots filled with something to eat, and if you were hungry, you ate. As for my gay cousin and his lover, I observed their patterns and behaviours for several years. I saw how others in the family treated the two of them, just like any other couple. Finally getting the courage and finding an opportunity (which was the other problem) I came out to him at 15. It was just a moment. I had to wave him into our front bedroom, when I was alone (a rare instance when you share it with brothers) as, too, the kitchen was the center of the house and adult's beeline for it upon entering our home. My grandparents were old school and believed children were not supposed to be in grown up's faces or business. It was so liberating to finally say those words to another person. "I'm gay." Particularly edifying when saying them to someone you know and love, who reflected that affection back to you. I would not say those words again to a family member for over a decade.

At sixteen years old, I began my first (and only) job working as a page, an entry-level position, in what would become a nearly 40-year career with the public library. This would start the steps of me moving slowly out of my shell into a wider world. Ironically, I discovered my love of libraries in Los Angeles, when my mother took us to a very large California library. I still recall the wonder I had. It would come around full circle years later in Louisiana, when I would inquire about a job at the local library. I walked past it going to school each weekday. My grandmother used to tease me by calling it my, "ten-cent job," but I know she was proud of me.

The day the phone rang, for me, it was the manager of the Epps branch. She told me to come in. My grandmother commented she had never seen a job call somebody before. What she may have not known was at some point I had stopped in and inquired about any job openings there. The manager remembered me because I was quiet and how I carried myself. I filled out the papers, went to the main library location downtown for an interview with the director, (my grandfather drove me), and I started that week. I was the only one of my siblings to get a job while in school. It would serve as the underpinning for my continued discovery of just who I was and that my life was very much an open book, in where I could take it.

The college years at McNeese State University, (MSU), started in 1983 but after one year there, and with little focus on what degree best suited me, and what exactly I wanted to do, I drifted. Work was still my base, along with home at the grandparents, whose push for higher education found me entering Sowela Technical Junior College in 1984. I earned a word processing diploma. It was something but I still always felt I disappointed the grands, and myself, not finishing MSU. You see, I was the first child in my immediate family ever to both graduate high school and to attend college. I just did not have a clear picture of what I could be. It would be 2000, Y2K, and a seminar called "Life Design" that helped me create goals, one being to re-enter McNeese. I did so while working full time and taking classes half time. I remained focused, maintaining my GPA, until I garnered for myself an associate degree and a bachelor's degree. My seven-year sojourn finally ended a journey that started 24 years earlier. It was another life event that reinforced my belief in myself and my own worth.

I would not square my gay life in Lake Charles immediately, which like the gay community itself, was mainly under the radar. My family and I never talked about it. It was for me some unspoken thing. My only source of the gay life I dreamt of was one or two gay bars that existed at any given time. I recall my first time walking into a bar; The Lawrence Street Pub. It was a small neighbourhood bar in downtown. It felt safe for my formal entry into the gay nightlife. I went with two friends who took me for my birthday. I quickly discovered the downtown area was teaming with gay men. When I was 19, I would ride my bike down to the lake front and found myself bike routes through the city that would safely take me there off the beaten path. This was my attempt to break free from whatever restrained me, to discover my independence and explore my world. This slowly but surely brought some older gay men into my life, as they would see me passing their neighbourhoods weekend after weekend. A wave here, a hello there. Once the door was opened, I would meet other neighbours, or friend of a friend and before I knew it, I was not alone anymore. Growing up I always believed I would have to move to some larger city, a New York or San Francisco, to find "community." Little did I know it was right here. Those were good, fun years, discovering and finding affirmation. Back in those days you could leave your doors open, everyone said hello and people seemed to watch out for their neighbours. One step leads to two and eventually I would be clubbing at Crystal's downtown bar at the end of the 80s, finding a gay world existed. I was no longer the only one in town.

Discovery of my untapped gifts and developing talents soon came in the form of acting. Theatre struck me like a bolt of lightning. I began backstage work in the Spring of 1993 at the Artist Civic Theatre & Studios. It would be here I fell in love with musical theatre and slowly found I had the 'acting bug.' Each thing helped me hone my craft in the local community theatres, then the college theatre, musical and non-musical productions. It was a surprising and safe place to find new facets of myself, by exploring other characters. I grew exponentially, auditioning for, and earning principal leads (or pivotal character roles) in outstanding plays like "To Kill A Mockingbird," "Jesus Christ Superstar," "Driving Miss Daisy," "Angels in America" and "Lilies of the Field," to name a few. From the latter production, I would win an ACTA award for my performance in 2012. I cherish any awards of recognition that I received over a lifetime, they come so rare to me making them more precious. Even in secondary school the rare trophy I earned (for choir, though I had received certificates for my grades) meant so much, helping bolster my spirits. After the turn of the millennium, I would film television commercials and record radio commercials. I managed to get a couple movies under my belt, including a remake of "All the King's Men." The likes of Hollywood actors Jude Law, Sean Penn, and the late James Gandolfini were brought to Louisiana, and across my path. Those may be stories from such endeavours, worthy of the telling on another day.

These things would fill up my life over the 16 ½ years between my first year and my final seven years at the same local university, even while the search for love, never far from my mind, eluded me. I became active in numerous groups and organizations, serving on the boards for agencies like the Southwest Louisiana AIDS Council, Mardi Gras Southwest Louisiana, and the Society for Creative Anachronism Inc. I was an active member of the (MSU) Banners Series Committee, The Ad & Press Club of Southwest Louisiana, and the Louisiana Choral Foundation with whom I sang. This lauded me with publicity and notoriety within the lake area that gave me a sense of worth and pride. I felt like I was doing things, things that mattered or made a difference. After two decades of volunteering activity the "Red Ribbon" Award was created and dedicated to me as its first recipient, by the Southwest Louisiana AIDS Council and presented by the Mayor of the city. Performing, volunteering, getting involved in the city, none of these were things growing up I ever had on my radar. Growing up poor in the black community other things ranked higher, like just living and trying to better yourself through education, but life is strange and wonderful with twists and turns, from the lemons of my childhood, I made lemonade.

Whether or not the world knew about my sexuality, or my condition, I did not ponder too much. I was just me. I carried myself in a way that people seem to like, perhaps earning some modicum of respect. The fact is I am a man of colour, in the South. I stayed out of trouble and kept my nose clean (avoiding alcohol, drugs, cigarettes, and any violence that would serve as run-ins with law enforcement.) On some level as I became an adult, I knew that my public behaviour could be discerned as a role model. I would have people affirm that, at times, telling me that they used my story to encourage others. My grandparents taught us to be men of our word, to carry ourselves in a manner, with dignity. I was one of a small number of black men in my community who were known beyond just the black community where I lived; known for being active and doing positive things in the city. Over time my legend here grew particularly with one special gift.

A dear friend, Yolanda Blanchard, will always be credited with me developing my journey as a storyteller. Over thirty years ago, at the end of the 80s she would come into my library life and (without knowing it) model for me how to bring stories to life for children. I would watch her effortlessly create wonder in them, every moment, until she spread her wings like a butterfly, and left us. She sparked something inside me before I even knew it was there. She would become my mentor. With time, the talents I had for crafting stories, with my own flare, and my acting abilities fused, taking me higher in both respects. In a couple of years, I had built a reputation as 'the' children's Librarian within the parish libraries (years later becoming, too, a professional storyteller for the Louisiana Endowment for the Humanities.)

Whenever I could financially travel, I did. The gayness within me, my free-spirited nature, was like the call of the wild. Through a windfall (small cash inheritance through my maternal great grandparents) I took a couple of trips in my early 20s and that gave me a taste for people, places and adventures. So far, I have gotten to see about half the United States, the U.S. Virgin Islands, the Bahamas, Canada, Australia, and New Zealand over the past thirty years. Adventures exposed me to exciting new cultures, opened my eyes and heart, creating a more-worldly version of myself. Ultimately, my treks would lead me to my destiny. Mardi Gras in New Orleans, 2015 is where I would meet, court/date, and ultimately return to marry my Montanan husband 5-years later. Ironically, in 2015 he and I would go to San Francisco. It was my first time (just like Mardi Gras, I was experiencing a year full of firsts.) During that San Francisco trip was when the Supreme Court announced the right to marry for the LGBTQ community. The Castro district was truly alive. We even got ourselves on the evening news. For now, our plans are to remain active in LGBTQ issues and organizations (like Prime Timers Worldwide and 406 PRIDE.) We have been fortunate to have found love late in life, and now with my retirement in sight, we want to create a vision for us living, hopefully, happily ever after.

Gloria Jackson Nefertiti

Gloria Jackson-Nefertiti (she/her) is a breast cancer survivor, whose 2013 diagnosis provided the catalyst for her to come out as bisexual, sex-positive, and polyamorous (because that was when she realized just how short life is).

Gloria is one of the most recent recipients of the Grants for Artists' Progress (GAP) Awards, which are hybrid merit-and-need-based awards for BIPOC artists, through Artist Trust, a nonprofit organization that supports working artists of all disciplines in Washington State. Gloria's discipline was literary.

Since 2017, Gloria has been a conference presenter of workshops she created, such as, "Transcending Shame" and "We Do Not Live Single-Issue Lives (a workshop on intersectionality)."

Gloria became a published author in 2014 when her poem, "What is Home?" was chosen for the Poetry on Buses program as part of "2014-2015: The Writing Home Collection." And in 2017, lightning struck twice when her poem, "Give Me Water" was chosen as part of the "Your Body of Water" collection. The Boston Bi Women's Quarterly also regularly publishes Gloria's essays.

Gloria is a recent graduate of The Narrative Project's "Get Your Book Done" program, which provided valuable coaching, getting her closer to completing her memoir (anticipated publication date: December 2022) entitled, "A Different Drum: A Black, Autistic, Polyamorous, Mentally Ill, Former Fundamentalist Christian/Cult Member and Breast Cancer Survivor WHO JUST WANTS TO FIT IN."

Links Mentioned in My Bio:
Artist Trust (https://artisttrust.org/grants/)
Poetry on Buses program (https://poetryonbuses.org/)
The Boston Bi Women's Quarterly
(http://biwomenboston.org/newsletter/archive/)
The Narrative Project (https://www.thenarrativeproject.net/)

(Photo credit: provided by author)

Well, I Probably Sound Like a Broken Record

I had been with my boyfriend Peter for a little over a year. We had begun having issues in our (mostly) blissful relationship. Since we knew that things had changed between us, we decided to talk about it. Finally, Peter offered up the idea, "Maybe we should open up our relationship." This was more than 20 years ago. Today, such an idea would be described in the Polyamorous community as "Relationship broken; add more people."

The Internet was still fairly new in 1996. There were USENET newsgroups, and some local poly mailing lists. I was subscribed to the Sea-Poly (Seattle Poly) email list, that would sometimes announce upcoming events. This time, they announced the Poly Potluck, which took place monthly, at a welcoming and affirming Christian Church. We decided it would be a good idea to attend and see if we met someone.

At one point that evening—during a break between the potluck portion and the panel discussion—I began to glance at the magazines on one of the tables. I think they were "Loving More" magazines, from the organization of the same name, a non-profit Polyamory organization that had conferences all over the U.S. (Recently, I've had the opportunity to present at their conferences in Denver and in Philadelphia, but I digress.)

While I was perusing these magazines, a skinny, slight-of-build man came up to me and said, "So! Do you see anything you like?" We got to talking and I found out his name was Artie, and that he and his wife sold crafts at a Seattle bazaar. He was cute. I thought he looked just like Davy Jones, of the 1960s pop group, The Monkees. We had to go back to our seats because the break was over, and the panel (made up of an FMF triad with a baby), was about to start. Afterwards, Artie and I met up again; this time, he asked my boyfriend Peter how we met. As he shared how we met, I felt giggly and embarrassed at the same time, just at seeing how much Peter loved me. Before Peter and I left the event, I gave Artie my business card that said, "**Gloria Jackson-Nefertiti, Professional Model**."

Artie and I ended up seeing each other for nearly 20 years, and I wish I could say that it was all (or even mostly) good times. Unfortunately, I began noticing, at the beginning, words and behaviours that would be considered deal-breakers for me today. But at the time, I had no boundaries, and was quite inexperienced in relationships, even though I was in my mid to late-30s. I'm sure this is another byproduct of autism.

At the time, I had no idea that some of the things that Artie said or did were inappropriate. For example, I was shy and mostly unaware of social mores. (I was also unaware that I was autistic.) This is one of the reasons why I hardly asked him any questions. Interestingly enough, he took offence at that, because it meant to him that I was not interested in people; otherwise, I would be asking more questions, instead of him being the one doing the bulk of the talking.

When Artie expressed his disappointment with me and anger at my inability to ask him questions, he said to me, "I've finally resigned myself to the fact that you will never be interested in other people!" The incredible shame that I felt at that moment caused me to feel sick to my stomach and for my cheeks to heat up. (Sadly, that was only one of many instances where he felt it was necessary to shame me.)

When I was first in the process of getting to know Artie, I noticed early on that he seemed to have issues with being openly affectionate with me in public. Today, this would be a deal-breaker since my primary Love Language is Physical Touch. I also noticed early on that several of my friends and acquaintances seemed to have misgivings about him. For example, when I told someone that I was in love with Artie, but he wasn't in love with me, the person said, "Wow, that doesn't sound good to me."

Over the years, people have also mentioned the fact that they wondered why they rarely saw him, or why he hardly came around. I'm sure they also wondered why they rarely saw the two of us together in public, but they never asked. I made excuses and would say things like, "Oh, he's just kind of shy." (He isn't.)

Early in our relationship, I came across a Zen Koan (a paradoxical anecdote or riddle, used in Zen Buddhism to demonstrate the inadequacy of logical reasoning and to provoke enlightenment). It was a parable that resonated with me, called, "*If You Love, Love Openly*," and it goes like this:

> *Twenty monks and one nun, who was named Eshun, were practicing meditation with a certain Zen master.*
>
> *Eshun was very pretty even though her head was shaved and her dress plain. Several monks secretly fell in love with her. One of them wrote her a love letter, insisting upon a private meeting.*
>
> *Eshun did not reply. The following day the master gave a lecture to the group, and when it was over, Eshun arose. Addressing the one who had written to her, she said: "If you really love me so much, come and embrace me now."*

Artie was and is, an interesting person, and not in a good way. He would frequently jump to conclusions that would have me scratching my head. For example, after I had been seeing him for maybe a couple of months, I remember he and I were walking to his home, where I would finally get the chance to meet his wife, Lou. It was maybe a 2-mile walk (he walked everywhere). We got to his home, and his wife immediately hugged me. She was very friendly. I also met their housemates at the time.

When we sat down at the dinner table, something happened that just rattled me. Artie received some news and reacted in such a way that came across to me as overreacting, something he would frequently accuse *me* of doing. His wife said something like, "You know how Larry, the plumber, was supposed to come over today and fix the sink? Well, something came up and he had to cancel." Immediately, Artie's demeanour changed to rage, and he banged his hand on the table, HARD. It happened so quickly and intensely that it scared me. Nobody else reacted to it, which made me think that they were totally used to it. But I held him on such a high pedestal that I just tried not to think about this incident, even though it really bothered me. Maybe if I thought about it too much, it would cause him to fall off his pedestal.

A day or so later, Artie said something else to me that was strange. I asked what his wife thought of me. What was strange was when he just blurted out (as he was wont to do), "Oh, she said you seemed like you'd be a hard person to get to know!" My face dropped when he said that, and I became crestfallen and disappointed. But I was also disappointed in Artie because he somehow thought it was appropriate to say that. It never seemed to occur to him that my feelings would be hurt by that statement. An empathetic person who thinks before speaking would have probably said something like, "Well, she's just glad she finally had a chance to meet you." But you know, I learned over the years that not only is he the kind of person who blurts out whatever is on his mind, without thinking. I also learned, sadly, that not only does he not care whether or not he hurts me, but he's also a sadist.

There were three things that Artie knew meant a lot to me:

1) for me to hang out with him and his family on occasion.
2) for him to tell his daughter (who he says he's really close to) about our relationship; and
3) for him to invite me over once in a while to celebrate Thanksgiving with him, his family, and family friends.

Regarding Thanksgiving, Artie would constantly give excuses as to why he couldn't invite me over. Nobody had to know about the true nature of our relationship. Why couldn't he have introduced me as a friend? Well, I know the main answer: *racism*. I'm sure I would've been the only Black person there, something I'm sadly used to. But somehow, he just felt it was easier not to even invite me. Another answer is incredible *sexual shame*.

Today, there's no way in hell I can imagine entering a relationship with someone who is as critical of me as Artie was, or who feels such an overpowering need to criticize me and argue with me. He found so much wrong with me—that is, he definitely saw me as broken and needing to be fixed, as well as fragile and too sensitive.

Recently, I thought back about our times together, and over a period of nearly 20 years, I have very few memories of actually having fun with him; nor do I remember feeling safe and well-loved whenever we were together. He provided absolutely *no* companionship. And worse yet, he was no good in bed. That's not something I say about many people, especially not someone I have a long-term intimate pairing with. Now, I wish I could say that what we had was a "relationship," but it's hard to define something as a relationship when one party does the lion's share of the talking (not communicating) and calls all of the shots in the "coupling." Whatever you call our "relationship," it was all on Artie's terms.

We had a *parent-child* relationship, which would've been perfectly fine if it had been something that he and I had agreed to. I'll tell you right now, though, that there's no way I personally would agree to that because it's not something I'm into. But as they say in the fetish/kink community, *Your Kink Is Not My Kink, But Your Kink Is Okay (YKINMKBYKIOK).*

I just realized recently that everything I wanted, I had to beg for, and I still wouldn't get it. And no matter what I asked for, he always had a way of making me feel like I was asking for something completely unreasonable. He wouldn't just say "no," but he would give me this long-winded "dissertation" explaining why he couldn't give me what I requested. Then, after this lengthy explanation or lecture, he would say something like, "And so, for that reason, I don't think it's a good idea for me to say those three little words at this time." Or he would say something like, "And that's why I don't believe in therapists!" Of course, if you were to ask me why he doesn't believe in therapists, or why he's not comfortable saying those "three little words" (I love you), I would have to shrug my shoulders and say, "I don't know!" That's because by the time he'd get to the end of his long speech, I would've forgotten what I asked, but more than likely, I would have forgotten what *he* said.

Now, I sang in various Seattle choruses, and he came to see and hear me perform with them at least four or five times. I always loved that, especially since it was rare for anybody to see me perform. I remember one time during a rehearsal when a choir member said that her coworkers would be coming to our concert. I felt a little bit wistful because I wished I had more people from my life coming to see me.

The first chorus Artie ever got to see me perform with was the Seattle Women's Ensemble. When I was invited to join the Seattle Lesbian and Gay Chorus (with whom I sang off and on, from 2004-2008), Artie came to at least a couple of our performances. Finally, he also came to see me once after I joined the Seattle Women's Chorus.

It meant so much to me for Artie (or anybody) to see me perform—that is, until I learned something around the time that I finally stopped seeing him.

One day, Artie told me that his friend, Tricia (who also happens to be one of my Facebook friends), was going to perform in a burlesque show. Tricia was also a friend of Lou, Artie's wife. In fact, she used to show her crafts at the same bazaar where Artie and Lou work. But here's what really gave me pause (among other things): Artie and Lou were going to go to her show, along with their daughter and her fiancé, now husband, and a couple of family friends.

When he shared that with me, I thought, "Hey, wait a minute! How come whenever he'd come see me perform, he would always show up by himself; yet he brought a whole crew with him to see Tricia perform?" I mean, that made me wonder, for the first time, where he told Lou he was going whenever he left the house to attend one of my concerts!

Why, I would've been so tickled if he brought his family and friends with him to see me perform. That would've made me incredibly happy. Yet, throughout the "relationship," he always felt the need to keep me a secret. And by not talking about me, it felt as if I didn't exist. That's how he wanted it, which was *not* okay with me. Besides, I'm sure that Lou would've loved to have gone with him to some of my shows!

The fact that he felt the need to keep me a secret just wreaked havoc on my self-esteem, big time. It made me think that he saw something very wrong with me. He was obviously ashamed of desiring me sexually and of having a sexual relationship with me when there's no reason why that should have been embarrassing or shameful. Today, I can't imagine being in a relationship with someone who's embarrassed by my presence, because I respect myself too much.

Occasionally, people would ask me what I saw in Artie. I had to really think about that! I mentioned earlier that when I first met him, I thought he looked just like Davy Jones of The Monkees. In other words, he was cute.

In the early 2000s, however, my late husband, Al, said to me, "Wow, Davy Jones has been looking a little simian these days!"

To which I said, "Well, he is a Monkee after all!"

Ba-dump-bump!

One of the words I would use to describe Artie is "peculiar." For example, as long as I can remember he has always worn this thick maroon-coloured corduroy jacket, even during the summer. And because he wears it most of the time, it smells bad. It doesn't necessarily stink, but it smells musty. The jacket also has the severely square padded shoulders that come straight from the 1980s. He looked as if he belonged in a Michael Jackson video. The only problem is that he can't dance. Still, that didn't keep me from wishing I had the wherewithal to tell him to "Beat it!"

In the early 2000s, there was a political rally at a park not far from the bazaar where Artie worked. Somehow, I had heard that Artie was going to be there, so I decided to go, too. The plan was that I was going to surprise him. Well, that was a mistake, and an embarrassing one at that!

Artie was clearly not glad to see me at all. I had forgotten that every time we accidentally ran into each other in public, it would always feel awkward. He would never come right out and ask, "What are you doing here?" But it would be painfully obvious that that was exactly what he was thinking.

I clumsily stood around, watching him talking to other people who I assume were either coworkers or friends. And he would stand with his hands in his pockets, as he ignored me and pretended that I wasn't there. At one point, he went over to Lou because he had a question about the digital camera he was using. I didn't recognize her because she was wearing sunglasses and her hair was a bit shorter than when I saw her around ten-plus years prior. Not only did Artie *not* even bother to reintroduce me to Lou ("You remember Lou, don't you?" for example), but he didn't introduce me to his friends, either!

After I felt that I had had enough of the event, I decided to leave. Artie and I said goodbye to each other, but I didn't bother to try and hug him. What would be the point? He would've just stood there with his hands in his pockets. As I turned to leave the park, I remembered feeling incredibly sad. It didn't help that my husband, Al, was unable to make it to this event. I was looking forward to having him there, so we could share in the event together, and maybe talk about it on the way home. But having Artie seem bothered and annoyed that I was even there in the first place, on top of not having my husband there, was almost more than I could take.

Later that evening, I received an email from Artie saying that *it was good to see me at the rally*. When I read that, I thought to myself, "Oh! I thought he wasn't glad to see me. Maybe I misunderstood. I mean, it sounds like he was glad to see me after all." Actually, Artie was a master of gas-lighting, where he would frequently cause me to question my own reality.

He would treat me badly the rest of the year. But in December, he would give me a card that was blank inside, so he could fill it with the most loving and heartfelt thoughts about me. Whenever I'd receive one of those cards from him, I would just read and reread, drinking in the written sentiments. My mouth would also be hanging open because I was in so much awe of him, and I couldn't believe what I was reading. I would always say the same thing after reading his birthday cards to me: "Oh, wow! I guess he must love me after all!"

It's in those times that I really wish I had someone in my life who could've been just super blunt with me, maybe even to the point of being painfully blunt. That person would've clearly helped to snap me out of my denial phase. And whenever I would get ready to spout that nonsense where I'd say, "Oh wow, I guess he loves me after all," my blunt friend would say something like, "*love you*? He doesn't even *like you*!"

A few years later, I finally got up the nerve to tell him how hurt I felt when he ignored me at the rally, and that he didn't seem at all glad to see me. After I told him how I felt, he lied to me, in order to cover his ass and to make it my fault.

He said that the reason why he treated me the way he did is because first, I sneaked up behind him and threw my arms around his waist. I didn't do that, and even if I had, so what? How is that wrong? What I do remember, however, is that I came up behind him and gently tapped him on the shoulder, making little contact with him. I wanted him to know I was there, but I didn't want to startle him.

Artie then said something afterward that made it painfully clear that he didn't like me in the least. He said, "Oh, well when you walked up, people looked at me and went, 'Ugh, who's that?'"

Now, I'm relatively sure that the last time someone said, "Ugh!" when they saw me for the first time, was in the seventh grade! That is not something that adults (or most adults) do. I thought that was not only a fishy story, but an incredibly hurtful one.

I remember sitting there next to him (we were in a park near my home because I wanted to talk to him), completely confused and bewildered at what Artie had said. I knew that the circumstances did not go the way he said they did.

Then he walked me back to my apartment building, shoved his tongue down my throat and left. I don't even remember if he said goodbye.

I walked slowly into the building, feeling completely violated. I finally decided that I had taken all that I could, and I needed to break up with him. I mean, it had never been clearer, just how much contempt he had for me. I felt like a discarded piece of chewing gum under his shoe. Then again, I'm sure he would've held a discarded piece of chewing gum in much higher regard.

"*Love you*? He doesn't even *Like* you!"

After a week or so of mulling this over, I called Artie and said, "You know, I thought about what you had said happened at the rally. I know that things didn't really happen that way." He thought for a while and then said, "Okay, *maybe* that's not how it happened."

"Maybe that's not how it happened?" I couldn't believe the ease with which he was able to lie to me. But why on earth did he think it was necessary to spin such an elaborate (and not even remotely believable) lie? Didn't it occur to him just how hurtful it was for him to say those things? Or did he not care, because he doesn't have a conscience?

It became painfully obvious to me that he didn't like me one bit, or that he only wanted me for sex, since that seemed to be the only thing that he thought I could do well.

"*Love you*? He doesn't even *Like you*!"

TRIGGER WARNING: Implied Sexual Assault

In January 2009, I had lap band surgery for weight loss. I asked Artie to pick me up from the hospital and give me a ride home. That was a decision that I will regret for the rest of my life (if I allow myself to think about it, that is).

For some reason, I still thought of him as my partner, even though his actions showed otherwise. I remembered filling out the exit form after I'd had the surgery, and I think it asked about Artie's relationship to me. I just wrote "Friend," even though I wanted to write something different. I think I wanted to write something like "Life Partner."

I remembered telling Artie how I wished I could say that he was my Life Partner, and I wished I could just be honest with other people about our relationship. He said *nothing*. I mean, after nearly 20 years of the same behaviour, it should have been obvious to me that we were certainly not on the same page (nor had we ever been on the same page), but denial is strong. Somehow, I still held him up on a high pedestal, and I wanted to believe that we were a *solid* couple, when we were never a couple in the first place.

When Artie drove me home, he said he wanted to come in for a bit. I had assumed that since I had just had major surgery, he was coming in to help me, and to make sure I was comfortable and had everything I needed before he left. I mean, that's what reasonable people in my life have done. And I should know, because I've had many, many surgeries. But no, that's not what happened. Instead, as soon as I lay down on the bed, exhausted from the surgery and anesthesia, *he started taking his pants off.*

sigh

There was something that Artie would frequently say to me, over the years: "Well, I probably sound like a broken record, but when a woman is vulnerable–really shows herself to be vulnerable–I just find that SO attractive!"

Hmm. He must have found me extremely attractive, then.

I still find it shocking that after all I endured from Artie over the years, I still remained in a relationship with him, *for nineteen years.* Then again, my late Mother stayed married to my late Father for more than *sixty* years, even though she (along with me and my siblings) frequently experienced physical and emotional abuse. However, there were two major life events that took place in 2011-2012, showing me that I had no choice but to end our relationship.

Significant Event #1: In late November/early December 2011, Artie's wife, Lou posted several photos from their Thanksgiving celebration. There were about 10-12 people in attendance, but what's significant is *that I was not one of them.* Artie never invited me to spend Thanksgiving OR just hang out with him and his family. When I looked at those photos on Facebook (which was painful for me to do), I was overcome with sadness, along with feelings of being excluded and not good enough. I kept trying to concoct reasons and excuses as to why he never invited me over. But once I was honest with myself, though, I concluded that the reason he didn't invite me was because *he didn't want to.*

Significant Event #2: In June 2012, I travelled to St. Croix, Virgin Islands with my sweetie, Greg, where we spent time with his entire family (parents, siblings, nieces and nephews). His family may not completely get the concept of polyamory, but that didn't keep me from feeling totally included and accepted.

Additionally, there were also a couple of major catalysts that forced me to decide to end my relationship with Artie, something I knew I could no longer put off.

Catalyst #1: In a group on social media, there was a post that shocked me into reality. It was titled, "How acknowledged/known are you in (your) partner's life?" This reply to that post helped add to my epiphany:

> *I don't do closets or hide my relationships, and unless a relationship is truly casual, it's important to me that my partners treat our relationship as real and legitimate, and that includes social acknowledgement and some involvement in each other's lives.*

Equally insightful to me was this reply:

> *Non-acknowledgement is a hard limit for me, both giving and receiving, so my romantic partners are all the type that make a point of showing affection and acting "couple-ish" (even when there are three or more of us).*

I wished Artie and I did "couple-ish" things, and the fact that I don't seem to exist in his world is unacceptable. That has *finally* become a hard limit for me.

Catalyst #2: In another social media group, a post entitled, "When/how do you know it's over..." further opened my eyes. Someone replied and said:

> *If we've had the same difficult discussion about an issue that is detrimental to the health of the relationship more than twice and still nothing has changed, that's my line in the sand.*

In many of our lengthy phone conversations, we had rehashed a lot of the same issues, *ad infinitum, ad nauseam*, and nothing changed.

One day, I participated in a poetry workshop. I think poetry is something else that continues to help me heal. I wrote a really short poem contrasting my relationship with Artie to those with people who adore me:

GLAD TO BE HERE

> *This bus is taking me to where I'm loved and celebrated.*
> *I'm leaving the place where I was shamed and intimidated.*

> *I'm facing forward, with great anticipation*
> *of seeing my friends who greet me with elation.*
> - *Gloria Jackson-Nefertiti, ©Nov 30, 2013*

Shortly after I was diagnosed with breast cancer in December 2013, I received plenty of opportunities to accept help and support from others.

For example, a social media friend who I call "K" asked if there was any long-distance assistance that she could provide me. At first, I couldn't think of anything. Then, I remembered how much I loved her poems that she would consistently post on social media. So, I told her, "Actually, I did just happen to think of something. If you can write me a poem ... that would really encourage me." That was exactly what she did, and quickly! I remembered being so stunned and blown away by the beauty of it that it took a while for me to regain my composure. I just couldn't stop reading and rereading it! What really amazes me is that for years, I had said that Artie knew me better than anyone else did. That was only because we talked on the phone so frequently. And yet, even though "K" and I have never met in person, she seems to know me way better than Artie did. He always saw me as weak and broken, needing to be fixed. As you will see in this untitled poem, "K" did not see me as broken or lacking.

I looked at her
for weeks without speaking
that kind of beauty
dries me up
words fail
in the hot
private ache
of admiration

So I looked
without speaking
it wasn't beauty only
some people

you can see the insides
from the look
of the outsides
and she shows
with a generosity
that plain steals
the breath from me
both

Did you ever see her?
a sunrise smile
a shape made for
compassion
something brave
and regal
about the set of the chin
it's not a face
built for ease
though there is in it
a great stillness
that like comfort
that is like wisdom
she's seen some things
and come back
and knows the story
and still
there is something
in the eyes
that is all warmth
and life
it was no wonder
People flocked
to draw
I thought
to sculpt
possibly just
to look

and come away
better
than when
they'd arrived

Go look now
you will, too

There are people
like that
not too many
I'm not sure we
could bear
too many
people who make
every one of us
bigger
just by their very being

I don't think that
she knows it
but I bet
we all the
rest of us
do

this wasn't going
to be a love poem
except they all are
and anyhow
when you see that
kind of grace
when you see her
kind of strength
you find true words
or none
and it was none

very nearly
until I looked again
at graceful lines
at all abundance
and sunrise
and found some

a near thing
that kind of courage
dries me up
words fail
in the hot
private ache
of admiration

Feb 21, 2014

Something that has provided me with great comfort is the fact that I have a vivid imagination that conjures up some amazing fantasies.

Revenge fantasies. I haz 'em.

Getting back to that political rally in the park. When it became obvious that Artie had strongly preferred that I not be there, I slinked away from the park, with my head down, and feeling completely worthless.

In my fantasy, though, I'm still slinking away from the park...at first. Then, I stand up straight, hold my head up, turn around, face Artie, and point my finger at him, while I say in a voice loud enough for him, his wife, and his friends to hear:

"You're not getting any more PUSSY from me, so don't even ask!"

There are several other fantasies, but I'll stop with that one. Besides, I'll never forget the day in May 2019, that I finally was able to get revenge on Artie. What was especially amazing and rewarding was that *there was so little that I had to do*. But that didn't keep me from feeling powerful and victorious.

But first, here's a bit of background. I'm an artists' model who comes up with imaginative poses for drawing, painting, and sculpture classes, mostly at schools, but sometimes, in studios. Some of the classes for which I model are adult continuing education classes, where some people will take the same art classes more than once because they like them that much. One night, a student in one of the adult continuing education classes at a community college, came up to me during a break and told me she was with the Seattle Rock Orchestra. She said that they had a concert coming up where they would be performing nothing but Beatles songs; specifically, it would be every single song from the albums "Abbey Road" and "Let It Be". She was telling me because she wanted me to have a free ticket. Yes!

Now, it just so happens that both Artie and his wife are *huge* Beatles fans; so much so that they even got married on the birthday of one of the Beatles. I won't tell you which one. I mean, you have four choices! And if you ask me if it's one of the Beatles who is still alive or one of them who passed away, I'll say, "Yes. It's Schrödinger's Beatle!"

Well, I went to the show, and I was so thrilled, Beatles fan that I am. I was singing along throughout the show, and when I wasn't singing, I was crying, and vice-versa.

After the show, I walked up to the stage so my friend would see me. She came up to me and we hugged, and I had a chance to gush about how much I enjoyed the show.

Then, out of the corner of my eye, I saw Artie! Even though I've known for years that Artie is such a big fan of the Beatles and their music, it never occurred to me that I'd see him at this show; probably because I ended my relationship with him six years prior, and to be honest, I really wasn't thinking about him *at all* when I made plans to attend the show.

Just the same, when I saw Artie, I thought, "Oh, no." I knew I didn't want to talk to him. However, there were *three* things that, had all of them been in place, I would have been glad to talk to him:

1) Artie needed to be smiling. (He wasn't. He was just staring at me, looking terrified. He seemed to be faced with a dilemma: "How can I talk to her alone when my wife is here?")
2) He needed to be standing closer to me, like six feet away (instead, he was hovering more like 10-15 feet away); and finally:
3) His wife needed to be standing next to him.

But *none* of these three things were in place. Still, I made some quick eye contact with him so he would know that I saw him. I made sure of that! After my friend and I finished talking, we hugged one more time.

When my friend left, I was alone.

But instead of talking to Artie, I turned and walked down the aisle and through the lobby, headed out the door, and caught a bus to go home.

Gloria has left the building!

Jayantha Withanage

I am Jayantha Withanage from Sri Lanka and have been living in Canada since 1996. I like to spend my time watching TV/Movies, doing work-out, cooking different kinds of food and travelling. I have been with my husband for 36 years and live in Vancouver, British Columbia.

(Photo credit: provided by author)

Jay's Story

I was born in a remote village in southern Sri Lanka in 1954. I am the eldest child with two sisters and one brother. Both my parents were government workers, and because of that we had to move from one place to the other every five years.

At that time, growing up as gay boy was not easy in Sri Lanka. No one talked about it, and even the Buddhist Religion did not mention anything about the subject. We did not have any magazines, books, or photos about queer culture. Movies were similar, only foreign movies had some images or storylines about Queer People, but all were highly censored. I eventually found some stories about Queer People by reading English novels.

In Sri Lanka's capital city, Colombo, where I eventually moved, there were some small bookshops with lots of English novels. These were very popular places to get novels about any subject, especially books with some queer content! It was at one of these places that I was able to buy my first book with gay subject matter, and read it within a week. We had to pay a kind of price difference as some books had higher lending charges. So, when I finished reading every book, I returned for another one.

Although I could not remember any titles, I enjoyed reading foreign books. The local library did not have any English books and Sri Lankan books did not contain any queer content. Those book shops would also let you look at sex magazines for a fee. But not gay ones, although it was still worth it to see nude guys that way! It was by reading those books that I learned about Queer Life, S&M activities, and bisexual culture.

It was very difficult to find a job in Sri Lanka. Political parties controlled the government jobs, and without their approval no one could get a job there. If someone supported certain political parties during elections, that person could get a post in the government job market. As I was not particularly political and did not support any parties, I was jobless for five years!

However, I eventually managed to get a job as a trainee, working in all areas of a tourist hotel in the city of Colombo. I was twenty years old, and I wanted to explore more queer culture, but I could not find anyone to talk to. So, I planned to go overseas to learn more.

However, due to the political situation in Sri Lanka at the time, leaving the country was not very easy. During that time, many young people wanted to go the Middle East for higher salaried jobs. But going overseas was a complicated process.

First, we had to bribe agencies to get working visas to Arab countries. Plus, we had to have police security clearance, and a Village Officer's letter. This letter was like a reference document indicating the person had no criminal record and lived in his village. It required a person's full address, their signature and the Village Officer's signature, plus a rubber stamp seal would be placed on the document. This letter was valid for three months only.

I also needed a letter from my new workplace confirming my new position, along with a passport authorizing me to work in those countries with my job title. One also had to provide a medical report, and a letter from one's village church or temple to prove your religion.

In the meantime, I was meeting lots of gay people from the United Kingdom and Germany while working at the hotel in Colombo. They would tell me about the freedom they felt as Queer People in their countries. They told me about freely available gay magazines, sex clubs/saunas, and parties without police raids! And although we did not have that kind of freedom in our country, I did meet some gay guys while working in the hotel at that same time.

In Sri Lanka, when people found out that you were single, they would ask personal questions, and others would spread rumours about you. To keep the questions and rumours quiet, and to "protect the family name," many Queer males felt they had to marry women. I knew that option was not for me.

I was happy to find lots of other gay people in Colombo. But the only places available to meet other gay men were in public toilets. In those days, public toilets in Colombo were very popular cruising places. Although they were not very safe due to police raids and pickpockets. However, some enjoyed these kinds of places. Old, young, government workers, and other people frequently cruised these toilets, but had to be very careful as lots of people come to use them all the time.

Some users ignored the things going on there, while some of those who cruised were shouted at. But many were into a quick masturbation sessions, or blow-jobs which were going on day and night. Interestingly enough, even some of the policemen cruised there! The toilets were a good place for some just to meet other Queer men. Since we did not have phones, and since we wanted to keep things private, and yet keep in touch, we exchanged addresses.

Since the toilets had no doors, it was very difficult to hide from others. Young boys who were hustling performed blow-jobs for money in the nighttime. There were less people during the night, so there was less of a chance that they would be harassed.

It was at that time, with the help of one of my friends I eventually managed to get a job in Saudi Arabia.

This is one of the strictest Middle Eastern countries regarding most things including alcohol consumption, and especially gay activities. Anyone caught having gay sex would face harsh punishments: jail sentences, deportations, and even death were common ways of dealing with Queer People. Because of that fear, all the queers had to be very careful, and I felt I had to hide my queer identity all the time.

I was working at a military camp in a small city called Taif, when I met my life partner. We both had a feeling that we were gay, so we introduced ourselves to each other, and as we talked we knew we were attracted to each other. As it turns out, he was an instructor at the English Language Department at a local university.

The military camp was very strict, and there was not too much mingling. Each nationality stuck to each other's groups, especially going out during meal time. We did not visit others in their rooms, and we hung out with our own countrymen. If someone was seen with another national in public, that alone could start a bad rumour! Some thought you might be asking for special favours like borrowing money, or trying to immigrate to other countries. But we managed to see each other at night very secretly.

We had been seeing each other for a while when we made a trip to visit my family in Sri Lanka. But we did not mention our relationship to anybody. We wanted them to believe that my partner was just a friend of mine visiting the country.

We eventually planned to get permanent visas to go to the USA and live there. However, it did not work out for us. When I went for my student visa at the US Embassy, it was denied. I was told that it had been denied due to Sri Lankans never returning to their country once they landed in The States. I ended up in Sri Lanka again.

My partner found another job and moved to Saudi Arabia again. One of my friends helped me to get a visa and I went to Bahrain. In Bahrain there were bars, clubs, cinema halls, not like the situation in Saudi Arabia. Although my partner was in Saudi Arabia I could not visit him, as Asians would not get visitor's visas, but Americans could come and go without any trouble.

Although we were still living apart, he visited Bahrain as I could not travel to see him. After a few months, he got a job offer and came to work in Bahrain and we were together again!! We stayed three years there.

After that he found a job in Dubai, UAE, and he helped me to get a visa to live there. We lived together for another five years. Still, because Islamic countries do not like queer culture, we were very careful about our relationship. It was then, that we decided to apply to get permanent resident visas to Canada. After lot of paperwork, I went to the interview and got very positive results about my application. After waiting over 18 months, I got my visa to come to Canada!!!

Even though I was very happy, I had doubts about our future together in a new country. My partner's job was not in the skilled workers' category, and the Canadian government did not need Americans to apply for positions that Canadians could fill at the time. So, we spent as much time together as we could.

Then, we eventually found out he could apply under the humanitarian visa category. We went to an interview at the Canadian Consulate in Seattle. We provided letters we wrote to each other, travel photos, travel video tapes, everything we could think of to prove we had been together for a long time. And after some months he got a permanent visa to Canada.

We married on July 20, 2005, exactly the day Canada legalized same-sex marriages by chance! This year 2021 we celebrate living together for 35 years. We are thankful for queer elders. Without their struggle and demonstrations, we would not be able to live as a gay couple freely in this country.

During those years spent in Sri Lanka and The Middle East, I never had dreamed that one day I would be living with my same-sex partner freely. Unfortunately, in Sri Lanka, anything Queer is taboo even today. But, we now live without fear of harassment or the need to hide our relationship from people or the government. Although our situation is still not welcomed in Sri Lanka and some other countries, we are happy to be here in Canada.

Oscar Hall

Oscar Hall was born in Nova Scotia in 1963 to hardworking parents and four older siblings. He moved out to British Columbia when his father retired from the Navy and his mother longed to be back in her home province.

Bi-coastal, bi-racial, and transgendered, he seeks to know his ancestors and himself as he learns to walk the red path.

(Photo credit: provided by author)

I Contain Multitudes

All my life I have yearned to be accepted;
loved for who I am.
My life was fractured from the get-go.
When I was born, I was alone in an incubator for the first month of
my life.
Is it any wonder that my health routinely forces me to return
home?
To my incubator. To my isolation. To my family.
To that which I first learned:
I'm not good enough, I'm not enough. I do not fit.
I do not belong.

Don't get me wrong, I did have a family and a
designation...female.

"Do I contradict myself? Very well then, I contradict myself. (I am
large. I contain multitudes.)"

I am borderless.
I fill and spill out of my cup.
Overflowing; I reject definition, limitation.
I cannot be named, bred, and labelled.   How could they know
who I was?
I fought to be alive and be distinct and whole. Not broken.
And yet I was. Am. I return to my incubator daily and cling on
to Me.
I am not my birth certificate,
not my resume,
not my obit.

I'll Pass

I must have been all of 5 when I heard my mother talking to her friend about me. Hearing my name roused my attention while I was playing with cars on our kitchen floor. I was immediately drawn to the conversation. I mean the subject material was fascinating. What kid could possibly pass up on an opportunity to hear about oneself?

What strikes me, in retrospect, was the tone of the conversation. My mother's voice sounded explanatory and embarrassed at the same time. There was confidence in her statement - a sense of finality to it yet speculative.

Upon hearing my name, I climbed up onto my feet and snuggled against Mom's side. I think she ruffled my hair and put her arm about my shoulders playfully. I smiled at them both. Tell you the truth, I don't remember who my Mom was having coffee with. Then the words she spoke reached my brain, "She wants to be a boy. I guess she's a tomboy."

I went back to my game as that seemed to be the conversation clincher and nothing about their new topic interested me. I never caught the prelude to Mom's comments. Was I doing something particularly "tomboyish" at the time? I just don't know. Her words have played in my head ever since. I don't know if my mother could have understood the profound effect they had on me.

Shortly after, I took to wearing a pair of socks in my underwear. It felt kinda good, natural but frustrating. Why? At the time my little brain had come up with a plan to fix how I looked physically to match how I felt inside. I knew about penises from playing doctor with some neighbourhood kids my age. My curiosity landed me in Mom's bad books most of my life and that was one of the times I knew I had let her down. It was around the same time as her statement but I don't think it was causal. Maybe it was. Perhaps the little me missed the connection?

Anyway, on one of those occasions my older sister caught me putting socks in my drawers and in a sing-song, menacing voice danced around the room saying, "Marie thinks she's a boy" over and over again. I slunk behind a chair in the living room and took the socks out and hid them underneath it. Later that evening while our family was watching TV, the doorbell rang and her taunts changed to "Marie, your boyfriend's here". Another kid in our block was over asking me out to play. I was so embarrassed. I got so mad at my sister. He was not my boyfriend. I didn't have a boyfriend. Samantha was the one that made my heart beat faster and not this boy! It seems to me that I had already internalized homophobia and didn't like the idea that I, a boy, could be interested in another boy. Had I got the message already that it was better to be a boy than a girl? Maybe.

Well, as I said, my mother's words had landed in the fertile soil of my curious little brain and I mulled them over. Was she right? She had said it with conviction and being the older of the two of us, I gave her the benefit of the doubt. Perhaps that's how people like me were defined. Okay then, the words sunk deeper into my consciousness. One thing was clear, "boy" and "tomboy" were not the same thing. The latter sounded dismissive, merely an inadequate, though acceptable, version of the former. Don't get me wrong, I could never have articulated this impression but I felt it. The meaning became embedded in my DNA. Whatever I was, I was not whole. Clearly, I was unhappy with who I was and wanted to be something else. Clearly, she was unhappy with who I was and wanted me to be "normal". You know, upon reflection I don't think unhappiness had entered my world yet. Well, now it had.

You see, before these fateful words I had never thought to define myself. I'd had no reason to categorize myself like a library book but others seemed to better understand me if I did. So, I started to refer to myself as a tomboy and everybody seemed happy. Until hormones kicked in and "tomboy" no longer fit. It seemed I now had to choose, "boy or girl?" That felt so claustrophobic, inadequate, and unacceptable. I couldn't breathe.

But more about that later.

So, as I was saying, I had never sought to define myself, there was no reason to. Who I was, was self-evident and inexplicably whole. I was much. I was limitless. I was sun. I was creative. I was smart and funny and so cute. Words could not define me, only experience of me could do that.

(TRIGGER WARNING: Implied Sexual Assault)

In the summer of my 6th year, I experienced another blow to my ego, to my being, my soul. I was raped by an older boy that was visiting a neighbouring family. He did it in a fort while all my friends were there. For some reason, when he started the others cheered and urged him on. Only Samantha seemed to have some adverse reaction to it. She ran into the woods crying. When he stopped, I quietly left the crowd as they focused on something new. Without thinking how, I found Sam hiding in a bush crying. We didn't say anything to each other, we both just cried. Sometime later we came out of the bush solemnly holding hands ... but something about "us" had changed and we both felt it.

When I was around twelve years old my older sister, Gail, was involved in gymnastics. I'm not sure how, but a family friend's young nephew (about five years old at the time) got the impression that my name was Jim Nastics. He was frequently told that Gail was at "gymnastics" which he took to mean she was with me. One day I arrived at our friend's house and the little guy was visiting. It was one of the times I had been forced into wearing a dress. He took one look at me in my dress and asked, "Jim Nastics, don't ya' want to be a boy no more?" Laughter ensued. But, I left feeling shame and confusion.

Some might say he truly saw me. But I wrestle with this because it shows how he chose the label that he thought best suited me "boy". At the time, I was just glad he didn't see the girl in me. Why was this a relief? Why did I feel shame?

As a teenager in Grade 8 I was punched in the face. I was standing up to a bully in our group and he said, "Since you wanna be a boy, I might as well treat you as one" and before I knew it, his right fist was connecting with the side of my head. He was stronger than me so I knew if I reacted things would get worse. None of my friends tried to defend me or discourage him in any way. This hurt. Not only had I had to suck up the indignity of being hit, I was once again left feeling embarrassed for having my masculinity recognized in a humiliating way. Once again, I was not acceptable. Once again, I was struck with the message that I was a "wannabe" not a whole person. I understood that when I was masculine I was disgusting and when I was seen as a girl I was vulnerable to violence. Why? It was so unfair and I had no one to turn to for support. I had no "Sam".

I remember Nancy. I was 13 and she was 12. A friend's sister. I had such a crush on Nancy. I only got to see her every other weekend as she only visited her dad at those times. After that first weekend visit, I was smitten. We laughed, chased each other, and sheepishly caught ourselves watching the other. It was so much fun and so natural; no awkwardness. It seemed forever waiting for the next visit. Finally, we were together with our friends and her siblings going swimming at a pool. When I followed her kid sister into the girl's changing room her sister asked what I was doing and giggled. Nancy laughed teasingly saying I'd better go into the boy's changing room and not try to follow them. When I told them I was in the right spot, the air in the room seemed to stale. Suddenly, a fun time swimming turned into a painful, awkward day. I got a crash course in what to expect over my teen years and felt sick to my stomach. She had been smitten with me when she thought I was a boy. But, how would she feel now that she knew I had this "girl" side of me too. I had been happy. I thought she saw me for who I was in my complexity and that all was good. Now public opinion had its say. How would she feel? Would she still like me and if she did, would she be forced to endure the judgement of others as I had? What if that would be too much? What if she suddenly put me in the "friend" category now that she had more information about me? Of course, all these questions were left unspoken and unanswered. I was awash in self-loathing and misery. Over the course of the next year my infatuation grew. She acted cautious around me. Most of the time she would keep her distance. On rare occasions, she came to me and we were physical. We never talked about those times.

I started having my period when I was 13. I was playing street hockey with a bunch of kids when someone suggested I go to the bathroom. I looked down and saw blood. I ran as fast as I could into my house hoping no one else would notice. I'm not even sure how I got to the bathroom and what I hoped to do about it. Somehow my mom found out what was going on and she showed up at the door asking me if I needed help. Did I know what to do? Though I had no clue, I wasn't going to admit it. Mom told me to look under the sink for a sanitary pad so I did. They weren't the modern type that sticks to your underwear. I had to figure out how to secure the pad. Filled with embarrassment and anger, I cleaned myself up. I don't remember much else about that time.

A sense of injustice, shame, and self-loathing settled on me and stayed there for years. Why did I have this body? The next time I went out to play hockey, the boys seemed to treat me differently. They were dismissive of me and gave me a wide berth. They were no longer my peers. I felt so lonely.

And then my family moved me from my home on the East Coast all the way to the other side of the country...to B.C.

I was depressed. I stayed up all night most nights. I listened to pithy music filled with angst and unrequited love and sang out at the top of my lungs. I ached to be accepted, known, and loved but I closed myself off from the world. Though friendly, I kept to myself most of the time. It was less complicated and more comfortable being alone. When I was around other kids I felt vulnerable and always questioned whether these kids truly liked me and I constantly doubted their friendship. Like most teenagers, I was trying to figure out my identity and how to navigate in a world that kept trying to fit me into some kind of mould. The message I got was, as is, I did not fit in. Somehow my lack of fitting in caused some kind of rift in the fabric of the world and people were desperate to rid themselves of it. I tried to guard my behaviour and mannerisms in order to "pass" as normal. It felt awkward. I felt lost and inauthentic.

My adult brother was going to his church one Sunday and I decided to go along. It was an Evangelical church and the minister called people to the front who were tired of feeling shame and wanted to be loved and accepted by Jesus. I went. This seemed a cause for celebration in my home as my parents, my brother, and sister-in-law lauded my "change". I'm not sure what they thought, other than I was no longer going to hell. But thus, began a new era in "fitting in". I spent the rest of my teen years studying the bible and seeking to be freed from my sin – that of being a lesbian. I didn't really have another term that seemed appropriate and I'd never met anyone like me before. I tried to date boys, then men. I always felt awkward and uninterested. I could not picture a future where I truly belonged. I shared my quandaries with my best friend who happened to be my minister, Evan. Before that, he and I had developed a kinship and appreciation for each other and had many interesting conversations. He had invited me to participate in ministry outreach and music. A part of me felt like I had finally someone around me who saw I had something to offer the world. After I told him I was a lesbian he stopped spending as much time with me. He started giving sermons on acceptable sexual practices. Where he had often encouraged my songwriting and musical abilities he now told me I would never write another song until I gave up being a lesbian. Wow....how could I do that? God wasn't changing me even though I begged repeatedly to be healed. Did he not care? Was he not strong enough? Did he not see the pain I was enduring? Well, if he didn't care, or couldn't help, or be understanding then he wasn't a god I wanted a relationship with. It was around this time that my parents started to tell me I was partly Indigenous. Mom seemed embarrassed by this. I later learned that her mother had tried to commit suicide because she could not accept my Grandfather's Indigenous family. While

Grandpa was lovely, the others were savages. This was the legacy she left my mother...judgement and shame. Sound familiar? Seven generations we carry these injuries.

I went to an "Unlearning Racism Retreat" back in my late 20's. It was only for people identifying as being female. At the time, I thought I was stuck in this category. No offence intended. Many who attended identified also as white. At the end of the weekend we stood in a circle and the host took turns standing in front of each of us and we were asked to say "I am a proud (Black, Brown, White, Indigenous) woman" thus accepting and celebrating our race with all its faults. When I said I was a *proud white woman*, my throat closed in on itself. I felt like a liar, a fraud, a cheat. I felt forced into saying something that wasn't true. I was embarrassed to say I was a woman. Although I now appreciate the feminine aspects to my being, at the time I felt shame. Here I was wrestling with fitting in as a lesbian in Vancouver and trying to understand if I really belonged. Here I was at a women's retreat feeling more lost and confused. Where did I fit in the world? Why was it so hard to feel safe and have a sense of truly belonging? Why did I feel like a liar and a fraud by identifying myself as White? I think because I carried my Mom's shame and fear of identifying as Indigenous; especially since my parents had not merely ignored but hidden the fact that I was bi-racial. I knew nothing about Indigenous culture and nothing about my family's history and ancestry.

It's crazy, but when I was coming out as gay, I thought other gay people wouldn't recognize me. They wouldn't see that I was gay. I didn't think I could pass as a lesbian. Did I even want to? "Lesbian" was too feminine and I was butch. Wasn't I? Isn't that how it worked? Still a binary system existed. I accepted I was Butch, not Femme. Except that as time went by, that logic started to crumble. I had no problem understanding how someone could be Bi, I couldn't figure out where I fit. It was later that I grew to realize that gender was fluid, not set, not stagnant. So now, on any given day, I feel more or less feminine or masculine. I still feel a pull to set the boundaries of my identity as though that is the only way I will ever be appreciated or understood. I identify as male but I am learning to accept the feminine in me.

Let me take you back to my early twenties. My family had started attending an Evangelical Christian Church around the time I went to church with my brother. My family started saying things like, "They should be shot, or placed on a deserted island to fend for themselves, or put on fire; they were going to hell" when talking about gay people. I don't think they had vocabulary or any understanding about gender diversity. Any deviation was defined as "of the Devil", evil, an abomination punishable by death. They would speak with disgust as though spitting the words out. I realized that they considered people like me disgusting. I often wondered if they knew I was queer at the time and if they realized they were speaking about me. I would pray every day not to be tempted by women. I would pray every day that God would heal me and make me right. It wasn't that I really wanted to be straight, but I wanted to be accepted and loved. Prayer didn't work. I headed back to the East Coast for a family reunion of sorts. My oldest sister still lived there with her family. All my siblings were going to be there as were my parents. As I boarded the plane to fly east, I was planning how I was going to come out to my family once and for all. That is until I was driving in the car with my mom and brother-in-law when they started saying those nasty hateful things. "They should be shot", said my brother-in-law. "Burn them", my mother said. I can't even remember how the "gay" topic had come up but their comments silenced me. I didn't feel safe. I felt afraid. Later that night I went out with my sisters to a bar for beers. They brought the subject up. They spoke positive words. It seemed they knew what I wanted to say and they seemed to watch me closely. My sister, Gail, talked about having a gay friend and going to a gay bar with her friend. Unfortunately, she said her friend protected her so women wouldn't keep hitting on her. At the time, I laughed even though I didn't feel like laughing. She seemed to echo the ubiquitous conviction that gay people were sexual deviants who prowled around for victims. I understand now that isn't what she meant. She spent the next few years hinting at how accepting she would be if someone she knew (looking at me) ever told her they were gay. But I let fear get the better of me and any thought of coming out slunk away to a deep, dark corner and didn't emerge until I had children.

As years passed I continued to feel separate, alone, unaccepted, unworthy, sinful, and ugly. I couldn't seem to get a handle on my attraction to women but tried very hard not to give into it. I had very limited intimacy. I kept finding myself attracted to seemingly straight women. I would tell myself it was okay to fall in love so long as I never acted on it physically. And, I promised myself to never "lure" a woman into my sin.

It was following one of my English poetry classes at college that I finally decided to "bite the grape". This was an image used by one of the poets we were studying to talk about the need to experience life fully – like rolling a grape around in your mouth but feeling too afraid to bite it, afraid that there was nothing more to enjoy once the fruit burst. (Walt Whitman, in his poem *Song of Myself*) I met an older woman who I thought was gay...my radar was on high on alert. I happened to be looking for books about coming out and her name popped up as an author of one. Her name and her picture were on the book, so I thought there was a good chance I was right. Right? So, I determined to tell her first. She became an encouraging confidant and introduced me to other gay people.

It's crazy, but when I was searching out my Indigenous heritage, I thought people wouldn't accept me as Indigenous. They wouldn't see that I was Sto:lo and struggling to understand and embrace my heritage. I was clearly White, as much as I was clearly a woman. Oh, how our bodies lie. I had no idea that in some Indigenous cultures being gay/lesbian was referred to as being "Two- spirited" and was not only acceptable but in some places even admired. I started going to Indigenous events like Pow Wows and community gatherings and celebrations. There certainly were people who I offended in my lack of cultural awareness. There were certainly times my ignorance was profound. I hoped that people would see I was genuinely pursuing my roots. Many did. Some did not. Many were patient and accepting. Some were not. Again, I wrestled with coming out. Again, I felt broken and unworthy. I felt ashamed to be White and felt pride in my Aunties and Uncles who, clearly Indigenous, had to survive invasion, confederation, unjust laws, residential schools, the 60's scoop, centuries of abuse and racial bigotry and did so proudly and with an inner strength I could only hope to approach. I was simultaneously mad at my parents for disavowing our history and family in efforts to be acceptable while also feeling proud of them for now searching out the truth.

I have spent years walking the Red Path and am slowly learning. I am learning about "Two-Spiritedness" and of medicines, of music and storytelling, and healing, and fires, and history. I learned who my people were and I am learning who my people are.

There is a park on the boundary of Mission and Hatzic, BC called Heritage Park. I spent many of my teenage and adult years walking through the woods from this park onto the grounds of the Residential School in Hatzic. I was comfortable in my own skin walking this land. I would carry my guitar and write music for hours sitting on this land. I would take my questions, my pain, and my hope there. In my late twenties, I fell in love while hiking with my first partner in these woods. In my thirties I went to my first Medicine Wheel under the care of Grandmother Mary, a Sto:lo elder. I approached from the east with the sun rising behind me. I crossed the field to the gathering where others drummed and welcomed the dawn. As sage permeated the air, as eagles soared above, as grass danced in the morning breeze wearing their morning coat of dew, I walked toward the fire, toward the people, toward the drumming, toward the future and felt I was walking home.

I used to work with a manager who liked rules and boundaries. She saw things in black and white. I always liked gray areas. I remember an email she sent out one Christmas. First, she acknowledged the festivity of the season and then asked people to bring in decorations. She demanded that the colours be limited to blue and silver. That seemed too controlled for me. I like variety and vibrancy. No one brought in decorations. Another time someone brought in their leftover birthday cake to share with the office. When the manager learned of this, she stormed into the kitchen yelling, "Who brought in this unauthorized cake!?" I think that desperate need to control the narrative, to demand people toe the line, to categorize everything and everyone is an attempt to manage fear and one's place in the world. In a similar way, I struggled to label myself in order to fit in, to be acceptable. I was desperate to find my place.

Nearing the end of 1999 I met a woman who would help define my "home" - a single mother with a pre-teen bi-racial daughter; a bi-woman; my hard-headed woman. With her I have learned so much about the world, my place in it, my identity, and about love and acceptance, my femininity and my masculinity. Vicky asked me about my dreams. How did I feel, gender wise, in my sleep, unconstrained by expectations? I had never seen myself as female. I had never thought about it. I was always male. I just was. Vicky was the first person I spoke to about being Trans. She said that was understandable. I had always sought to fit in, to pass, to be acceptable. Over the years, I have been able to refine myself with her support. I am learning to care less about the world's view of me. I care less about finding an all-encompassing authorized label. So, if anyone asks me to change or justify my identity, I think I'll pass!

I am a parent. I am a lover. I am bi-racial. I am a musician and a storyteller. I am Two-Spirited. I am.

Shinji Kasama

Shinji was born and raised in the central part of Japan. When Shinji was in his mid 20's, he met his American partner, who was teaching English in the country. The bi-national, bi-racial, same-gender couple lived in Japan, moved to the United States, and finally immigrated to Canada.

Shinji and his partner have become Canadian citizens, and the couple makes Richmond, British Columbia their permanent home.

(Photo credit: provided by author)

My Journey

Born in Japan

I was born in Japan in the early 60s, the youngest child of a large but ordinary family. I was sensitive and cried easily. I played outside with other boys a lot—but I didn't like playing sports. And, when I did play, my friends knew that I wasn't good at it, so they didn't expect much from me. So, at least I wasn't under any pressure to be an athlete.

I never thought much about my sexuality until I noticed something when I was watching some romantic scenes on TV dramas and in movies. I wouldn't wish to be kissing the girl, but I wanted to be kissed by the guy! In my adolescence, I realized that I preferred boys to girls and became increasingly attracted to some of my male friends.

In the early 70s in Japan, there was very little information regarding homosexuality. The only instances mentioned by the media were female impersonators in show business who were either eccentric or comical, or negative portrayals of gay characters in dramas. They were usually criminals or some kind of psychopath, and almost always met a tragic end. There were never positive images of gay characters or stories with happy endings. In short, I can't recall a single positive image of a gay character. As an early teen, I came to believe that I was not supposed to have romantic feelings for someone of the same gender. And it wasn't a big issue at the time, as I had other interests, like listening to music. I was also hoping to grow out of it, get married, and have my own family when I got older.

Adolescence

As I entered my late teens, my friends started talking about girls, and I pretended to be interested in them to get along with my friends. However, some boys were reaching puberty, and I couldn't help but have some attraction to them.

When I was in the 8th grade, a new boy came to my school. He was very flamboyant. He wasn't a big kid, but he had a loud voice and spoke with many feminine words and expressions. Also, he didn't hide his longing for one particular middle-aged male teacher. Despite his behaviour, he had a buzz cut and an aggressive personality, so he didn't fit the stereotypical gay image I'd seen on TV. He also loved to sing, and he started a folk-rock band, which many kids thought very cool. I admired his open and free character, but he was a popular kid and I was just a quiet closeted kid, so we didn't become close friends, at first.

At one school festival, he arranged to have a stage performance with his band, and he asked me to play the drums, as I was playing percussion in the school band. So, I did, and we became friends. He never asked me if I was gay, and I never told him. But he seemed to know. One day, he told me about a gay magazine he knew of. I was curious about it, but didn't have guts to buy a copy. A couple of years later, when I was in high school, I summoned the courage to buy it, and that opened the door to the underground gay scene for me.

As I entered my late teens, my desire for another man was getting stronger, and I was curious to meet other gay people. Even though my home town is small, it's not too far from Tokyo. So, I could explore some of the gay district I read about in those gay magazines—but I didn't find it very exciting.

The problem was, most of the ads in the magazines were for bars and some establishments where minors were not allowed, so all I could do was just walk around the area in the mid-afternoon on a weekend. I returned to the gay district a couple of times hoping something might happen or meeting someone by chance, but there was nothing. It was a total waste of my time and the cost of transportation, so I stopped going.

Young Adult

I went to college after high school, but I quit after a year and found a job far from my hometown. I met another gay person at my workplace, and one weekend, he took me to his favourite gay bar in Tokyo. Although I was old enough to enter and have a drink, I knew right away that bars were not my thing.

However, sometime later, I went to the gay district alone and visited the places I couldn't get into when I was a minor. I have to admit that I enjoyed the experiences there. On the other hand, I felt guilty for having a secret I couldn't talk about with my family or friends. I was also careful not to get too used to the scene. I didn't even want to make a friend in the gay community, because someday, I would stop coming to this place when I got married.

By then, both of my sisters were married and had started their families. My brother was dating his girlfriend. Even some of my friends had already got married. I also wanted to have my own family, just like everyone else. But would it be possible to find someone to get married to and have kids? I knew the answer was *no*, but I didn't want to admit it. In my fantasy, I would meet a nice guy and we would live some place alone. Wouldn't it be nice if a knight on a white horse rescued me? But I was too old to be dreaming about nonsense. In reality, I was alone worrying about my future but not knowing what to do.

Meeting Ed

After a couple of years of working away from home, I went back to my parents' place and started another job in Tokyo. One day, in October 1986, I was on my commute and I had to switch trains. While waiting on the platform I noticed a young white guy standing nearby. Since this station was in Yokohama, a major metropolitan city, seeing a foreigner wasn't unusual in the 80s.

I wasn't paying much attention to him, and when the train arrived, we got on through different doors. As was typical during Japanese rush hour, there were many commuters, and I had to move to the center of the car as more and more people boarded the train. As it turns out, this guy was also pushed to the center, until we stood side by side.

The train was a rapid express, and the ride was about 10 minutes to the next stop. When the train swayed, his hand touched mine. At first, I thought it was by accident. Then his hand touched mine again, and again. I glanced at him, and he was gazing at me! It occurred to me that he might be gay. I didn't know what to do next because there were so many people around, and I didn't speak any English at the time. So, when the train finally arrived at the next station, I took his hand to get off the train together.

Once out of the train the two of us stayed on the platform. He started talking to me in Japanese, which was a relief. His name was Ed, and we had a small chat. We got on the next train, and got off at the station near where he lived, and went to his apartment.

A few days passed, and I found myself thinking about him quite often. So, one night while taking the train, I decided to get off at the station near his home. I had no idea if I would see him again, but I knew he would get off at this station after his work.

The next train came, and people got off, but he wasn't there. Many trains came and went. Finally, I spotted him in the crowd of people disembarking the train. It wasn't difficult to spot him, as he was the only non-Japanese. He was a bit surprised, but he seemed to be happy to see me again.

I had a fairly busy life at the time, so Ed wasn't the only thing occupying my mind. But the more I saw him, the more I wanted to see him. We started spending more time together, and eventually, he gave me a spare key to his apartment.

Ed wasn't a cook, so he had only a few pieces of cookware and dishes. One weekend, we went to a department store and I had him buy more kitchen essentials so that I could cook something at his place instead of going out every time we would meet. The first thing he had to buy was, of course, a Japanese rice cooker.

Eventually, we went on a weekend trip to a small-town famous for hot springs, and we stayed in a traditional Japanese-style inn. That was the first time we spent more than a night together. After that trip, we discovered that we enjoyed spending time together, and by that point, we found that we enjoyed each other's company and began dating more. I had never met anyone I felt that close to, even though we spoke different languages and had different backgrounds. What was important to me was the soul in his body.

Turning Point

One summer day, I visited Ed at his apartment. He said he had something to tell me. He wanted to spend the rest of his life with me in a committed relationship. And if that wouldn't be possible, we should break up now, as breaking up later would be harder and more painful. I couldn't answer right away, but I sensed his seriousness in his voice, and I knew I had to consider his proposal seriously.

By that point, Ed was very important to me. He was the first person I had such a close, deep, and very personal relationship with. But I couldn't shake off the very Japanese way of thinking that I was supposed to get married and have my own family. Also, I was only 25 years old then, and I couldn't see myself making a lifetime commitment with another person, especially a man. I wasn't ready for that.

Had I been in a heterosexual relationship, I could have talked to anyone about whether I should make up my mind and get married or not. But being in a same-sex relationship, I felt I had no one to talk to about my relationship with Ed. Unlike today, there was no internet or chatrooms. Having avoided any connection with the gay community, I didn't have gay people I could ask for advice. It was a life-changing decision for me, and I had to ponder this decision alone.

The more I pondered, the more I became angry with him. I couldn't believe this American guy thought we could just live together for the rest of our lives because we love each other. Did he think we could live the way we wish and live happily ever after like in Hollywood movies? Well, I'm Japanese and I knew the importance of fitting into the society. There was no room for two guys living together like a married couple. I had never heard of such a case! What he wanted sounded totally unreasonable and truly unpractical!

For days, I thought about what I actually wanted in my life. If two guys were to live together for the long term, Japanese society is not an ideal place. In Japanese society, everyone is assumed to be like everyone else, so if you are a certain age, people will ask if you're married, and if so, how many children you have. From a Canadian's point of view, that's none of their business and very rude to ask such personal information. But most Japanese people think asking these questions doesn't seem to be rude or too personal, since everyone else is supposed to be married and have children by a certain age. Things may be different now, but some, especially the older generation, still ask these questions and even ask why you don't get married if you're still single.

I was in my mid-twenties, but I was male, so generally people didn't ask me too many questions regarding my marital status. But the social convention was such that men, (and especially women) should get married by 30 or so. And the pressure of expectation would be on not only me, but also on my parents. Fully aware of the social convention of the society, I couldn't imagine Ed and myself living together in Japan. Maybe we needed to move to the US.

Ed had to renew his work visa in Japan annually. He looked into applying for permanent residency there, but the stakes were very high at that time, unless one is married to a Japanese citizen. That meant I would have to leave my country along with my language, familiar culture, and food. I would have to give up my job, which didn't pay well but it was something I enjoyed. If I moved to the US, I would become a visible minority there, and I would have to learn English. I might not be able to eat some food I was used to in Japan. And how could I find a job there? The disadvantages were too great if I moved there. But maybe it would be much easier for us to live, since Americans tend to mind their own business. I wasn't sure, but at least life looked to be more open in the US than in Japan.

Then I had to ask myself, *Can I give up everything I have, pack and move to the US just to stay with Ed? Is it possible for two men to have a committed relationship and live happily together?* Eventually, I came to the conclusion that I *could* give up everything for him. I'd never heard of any long-term committed gay couple back then. I thought we were the only ones making such a commitment.

I visited Ed and I accepted his proposal, under one condition, he must take me to the US before I turned 30. His eyes lit up and he looked happy. We didn't have a ceremony or blessing, but we had each other, which was all we needed.

Living with Ed

Once we made up our minds and set our goal, we started looking for a place to live. We still had time until our move to the US, but in the meantime, we needed a place to live, as the apartment he had was too small for both of us.

We found an old Japanese house to rent in a rural area. It was a little far from our workplaces, so the commute took longer than we wanted, but the house was large and had a nice yard, which wasn't available in big cities. It was also located close to a beach, so we fell in love with the old house.

Coincidentally, the date we moved in was the day we met exactly one year before. Since then, we decided that that day is our anniversary.

After we started living together, we were just like any newlywed couple. I couldn't wait to get home after work, and enjoyed cooking our dinner. Sometimes, we met for drinks or dinner after work, and then went to a movie or a concert.

Afterward we went home together and I was happy that we didn't have to say goodbye after our dates.

There was a small bakery we liked near the rail station, and we used to shop there. One day, I noticed that they were selling pieces of cake at discounted prices. I couldn't just pass it by, so I bought two pieces each of two kinds of cake. I was looking forward to surprising Ed with those cakes. But once I got home, he surprised me that he had bought exactly the same two kinds of cake, and two pieces each! We burst into laughter, and we were also impressed how we would think alike so much!

We enjoyed our lives together, and one day, Ed gave me another surprise. He had saved money and bought an old car! It wasn't a fancy car, but we didn't need an expensive car since we were planning to move to the US in a few years. By driving, we were able to find more interesting stores and nice restaurants, and we also took trips together.

Years passed, we were getting ready to move to the US. Ed took me to see his parents and other relatives in San Diego. While there, we met an immigration lawyer one of Ed's friends introduced to us in San Francisco. For me to immigrate to the US turned out to be much harder than we expected, but most importantly, I had to learn English. So, I applied for a student visa, and Ed found an ESL (English as Second Language) program at San Diego State University.

Moving to the US

We moved to San Diego, full of hope for our future. I was already in my late 20's, and I became a student again. I enjoyed the new environment and studying English with other young classmates who were from other countries. I even joined a gay community band. Although I still couldn't speak much English, my ability to read music and play percussion helped me to connect with new people.

We went to a Gay Pride Parade for the first time. We couldn't believe how open they were, and how proud and out they were! There was a young police officer coming out at the parade, who made front-page news in the next day's San Diego paper. We were very excited and convinced that we had made the right decision to come to the US. Also, I was pleasantly surprised to watch a PBS documentary on lesbians and gays in the US, including same-sex couples! We were definitely not alone, and we weren't the first ones to have a long-term, committed, same-sex relationship! We were very encouraged.

While I was enjoying my new life in the new country, Ed was having a difficult time finding a job. He took me to his home country, so he felt all of the responsibility for us living together was on his shoulders. I wasn't earning any money, but spending our savings for my tuition. At that time, the economy in the US was not in good shape, so that didn't help him either.

To make the situation worse, I had a bad toothache. It turned out I needed a root canal. Since dental treatment in the US was formidably expensive, it was cheaper for me to fly back to Japan and get treatment with Japan's national health care plan. The good news was, Ed was finally able to find employment at a major US airline, which had just started to fly to Japan, and they were hiring new flight attendants who spoke Japanese.

Because it takes a long time to get dental treatment under the Japanese healthcare system, I had to fly back to Japan and stay there for a long period of time. In the meantime, I was able to get a part-time position at the office in Tokyo where I used to work. I enjoyed coming back to Japan, where I was so used to everything, but at the same time, I missed Ed terribly. International phone calls were very expensive then, so we rarely made phone calls. We mostly communicated by airmail, which took about five business days between Japan and the US. Some people say long-distance relationships won't work. But for us, even though we were in two different locations, we never felt apart in our hearts.

While I was in Japan, Ed went through training to become an international flight attendant, and he moved to Seattle, where he was based. I was a little bit disappointed that we couldn't live in California, which I rather liked. Seattle was a new place to Ed as well. In an unfamiliar place, he had to find an apartment for us and a new school for me to attend.

Once I got my dental treatment done, I flew to Seattle. I was more than ready to go back to the US, because my neighbours had started asking my parents if I was still single and suggested that I meet some eligible ladies.

The place Ed found for us was not actually in the city of Seattle, but in Bellevue, just a few blocks away from Microsoft's headquarters. I attended an ESL program at a nearby community college, and Ed was working as a flight attendant between Seattle and Tokyo. We started our new lives all over again.

We met great people and liked the new environment. In the northwest, there were many more community bands, orchestras and other music groups compared to California. So, I started playing percussion again. I was able to expand my network through my music activities, and I started feeling at home. With Ed being a new employee and me being an international student, we didn't have much money, but we still enjoyed our free time by exploring new places. Having lunch at a restaurant would be too expensive for us, so I made simple lunches and we had small picnics along the way. Not having extra cash didn't stop us from enjoying our new life in the new place.

But there was a big issue we couldn't ignore. I was there with a student visa, and that wasn't a permanent status. If we were a heterosexual couple, we could get married and I could get a green card, permanent residency, but we didn't have that option.

In the meantime, Ed had saved some money, so instead of paying rent every month, we decided to buy a house. Or to be more precise, Ed bought the house, as I had no legal relationship with him under US law. We, or Ed couldn't afford to buy property in the expensive Bellevue area, so we moved to the north. It was a new strata development just like a condominium, although each house was physically detached. We had a yard, so we planted roses, trees and shrubs we liked. Even mowing the lawn gave us a sense of satisfaction of home ownership. We also bought another used car, and I continued playing percussion with many groups. We were happy to see our progress since we moved to the US. However, there was always the underlying issue that I didn't have a permanent status.

Around that time, gay rights were a hot issue in US politics. The states of Hawaii and Vermont were even talking about legalizing same-sex marriage. An immigration lawyer we saw in Seattle had told us that if any state would legalize same-sex marriage, we would have a big chance and she would fight for us. So, we were hoping that either Hawaii or Vermont passed legislation to legalize same-sex marriage, which sounded like it could happen very soon. But the majority of people at that time were against it, and the debate was nasty and ugly.

One afternoon, I had a phone call from Japan. It was from my brother. He told me that our father wasn't doing well, and perhaps I should come home. I told him that I was coming home right away. After I hung up, I told Ed what was happening to my dad, and we knew what that meant to us. By that point, I couldn't extend my visa any longer, so once I left the US, the only way I could return would be as a tourist, which allowed me to stay only up to 90 days. I didn't want to leave the country before Hawaii or Vermont would make a historic move, but I had to go back to Japan before it was too late. I was sad that my father may not be with us for very long, but I was more devastated by another separation Ed and I would have to go through. And I hated and despised myself for grieving our separation more than my father's well-being.

Even on the day I had to leave for Japan, I hoped to hear the news of Hawaii or Vermont legalizing same-sex marriage. That never happened.

Ed took me to the airport, and I got on a flight to Tokyo. Even though it was a painful departure for both of us, we already had our next plan: immigrating to Canada.

Moving to Canada

Neither of us had any connection with Canada, but the idea wasn't new. When we lived in Washington State, we used to go to Seattle Pride. One year, a friend of ours introduced us to another friend of his. The new friend told us that he and his Thai boyfriend were immigrating to Canada soon, because he couldn't bring his

Thai boyfriend to the US. We also met people in a group called LEGIT. The Lesbian and Gay Immigration Taskforce. They were a volunteer group founded in 1991 in Vancouver. They came to Seattle Pride to talk about how to immigrate to Canada. We were intrigued by it, but we had just bought the house, and it seemed too uncertain for us, so we didn't pursue the possibility at that time.

Once I arrived in Japan, the first thing I did was to see my father in the hospital. He couldn't speak, but he was able to look at me, and he smiled at me, so I was so glad to see him.

I was already in my late 30s, and I was once again living in my parents' home, where my brother and his family had moved in to take care of my elderly parents. My brother and my sister-in-law warmly welcomed me, and their two young boys were happy to have an uncle they could play with.

My father passed away a couple of weeks later, and I found a temporary position at a Japan Post depot in the town. It was the night shift, but the work schedule was flexible, so it was perfect for me. Ed was still flying between Seattle and Tokyo, so whenever he came to Tokyo, I took a day off and went to his layover hotel.

By this time, e-mail was the main communication tool for many, but my family didn't have a computer, so I bought a computer with my first paycheque, and Ed and I were able to communicate much faster. It was a great benefit for us, because we were busy gathering information and writing a cover letter for our immigration process. Also, because of the time difference and my nightshift schedule, we were able to send e-mails when we were both at our computers.

Gathering documents and information, writing a cover letter, it all took time and it was tiring. Once again Ed was in the US and I was in Japan. My brother, not knowing the nature of my relationship with Ed, asked me why I needed to move to Canada. For him, Ed living in the US and me living in Japan seemed natural. I simply told him that Japan didn't suit me.

It took a long time to get our application ready to immigrate to Canada. Then we had to wait a longer time to hear from the Canadian government for our interview date.

In the meantime, I had been back to the US a few times to see Ed. Each time, my stay was not long, but with his airline passes, I was able to travel for a small fee. One time, an immigration officer looked at my passport and noticed I came to the US frequently. Since these trips were not work-related he gave me a difficult time. But he couldn't find anything wrong with my visits, and he let me through.

I was supposed to come back again to Seattle for our immigration interview at the Canadian Consulate, and when we got our interview date, I was nervous entering to the US again.

Fortunately, this time, I didn't have any trouble. We hoped that our interview would go smoothly as well. However, it didn't go the way we were hoping for.

The officer who interviewed us was very kind, polite, and professional. She impressed both of us. However, after evaluating our case, she could approve Ed, but not me. The way the system was set up was, points were given to candidates in categories such as: job skills, education level, etc. She told us that I didn't meet the standard and didn't have enough points.

My heart sunk. First, we left Japan because we felt there wouldn't be a room for us as a couple. Then I had to leave the States because I couldn't get a green card. Canada was our last hope, but I was rejected again. All we wanted was just to live together, but it seemed there was no place for us in this world. Tears came down and I started sobbing. The officer gave me a box of Kleenex and comforted me, but I couldn't stop sobbing. She tried to find a way to approve me, and she said she would re-evaluate my case for consideration on humanitarian and compassionate grounds. But the decision was to be made not by her, but by her boss. Therefore, we had to spend some uneasy days after the interview.

Days later, we received good news. I was approved, and we were delighted.

When I arrived at Vancouver Airport to become a landed immigrant, I immediately felt the belongingness to this place. I had visited Vancouver a couple of times before, but I was a visitor then, and this time I came here to become a permanent resident. It was a totally different feeling. Ed drove up from the States the next day to become a landed immigrant as well. It was in February of 2001.

We started our new lives in a new country. Since Washington State is only a few hours drive from here, we were able to sell the old place, and drive up here to find a new place to live. We bought a condo in Richmond when we became landed immigrants. Ed didn't have to quit his job, and continued working for the same airline by commuting from Vancouver to Dallas, where he was based.

After moving here, we met other same-sex couples like us; Americans who couldn't take their same-sex partners to the US. Two couples have become very close friends of ours, and we now regularly hang out. New place, legal residential stability, and new friends. We thought we got everything we needed as a gay couple. However, Canada gave us even *more* than we wished for.

Two years after coming to Canada, same-sex marriage became legal first in Ontario, and then in British Columbia. Since we had been celebrating the date we met, we decided to get legally married on our anniversary that year. We initially thought legal matrimony wouldn't mean too much to us, since we had already been committed for so long. We had a small and simple ceremony in the living room of our condo with two witnesses and a marriage commissioner. However, during the ceremony, we realized how powerful and deep legalization was. It was serious and solemn, and not to be taken lightly.

Now that we were legally married in Canada, we couldn't wait to become Canadian citizens. As soon as we became eligible to apply for Canadian citizenship, we didn't waste any time. When we received our Canadian passports, we felt like we had finished a long journey.

Now we were finally home.

In the years since we became citizens, Canada has changed its immigration law in ways that make it easier for couples like us. Even in Japan, many young LGBTQ folks have come out and become visible.

Times are different and things are changing. I hope to see a day when being LGBTQ is no longer a big deal, and everyone can be themselves just the way we are.

Agustin Restrepo

Born and raised in Panama City, Republic of Panama. Moved to the United States in 1979 and lived in Texas for 34 years. Attended Texas A&M University in College Station, Texas. Also, attended Houston Community College in Katy, Texas.

Moved back to Panama in 2013. Currently living in Colombia working as a freelance Landscape Designer.

Bilingual (English/Spanish) but can communicate in other languages. Eclectic background music, arts, activities (from sports to puzzles). Travelled extensively. Always have a positive attitude.

(photo credit: provided by author)

Agustin's Story

My name is Agustín Restrepo. I was born and raised in Panama City, Republic of Panama. Born into a bilingual, Catholic, middle working class, (meaning both parents worked).

My dad, the oldest son of Colombian immigrants, had five kids and a house in the suburbs with my mom by the time I came along. My mom was the second daughter of a family with eleven children. Together all eight of us (my mom, dad, my siblings and me), lived in a rather typical American-looking one-floor, chalet-style home in a typical looking late 50s, 60s, 70s style neighbourhood. Close families, houses without outside fences or walls, kids riding bikes, skating, playing ball on the streets without the fear of being hit by cars because of low traffic.

There were a lot of similarities between the world in which I grew up in Panama, and the one of my friends in the United States, and yet there were a lot of differences. One major difference is that I grew up in a segregation-free and racism-free society, while racism was blatant in the Panama Canal Zone back then. The Canal Zone being (at the time), a United States Territory, and was ruled by U.S. law, which included segregation. All the non-Caucasian officers and their families would be settled in communities within the Canal Zone Area, but outside the Armed Forces Bases. There was also a different pay status for White and non-White members of the armed forces. That was also the arrangement for contract labour.

Our school year ran from April through December. We would leave school around December 15th, and be off school until April. That would free us for the Christmas holiday, New Year, Carnaval, and Easter. This would give us plenty of time to go to the beach and spend time with parents, (some would schedule their vacations to coincide with the kids' school vacations). We would have activities like, for example, at the end of the year festivities, the neighbours would get together and decorate a vacant lot near our home with a Nativity Scene with lights and figures. At night, we would sing Christmas Carols, (Spanish traditional), and re-enact the nativity scene with local kids from our neighbourhood dressed as the characters from The Biblical Christmas Story. Rumour has it that I played the baby Jesus in one of the many re-enactments.

All the homeowners would install lights and Christmas decorations. Our neighbourhood's holiday display and show became so popular that local Catholic priests started attending to give a Mass during the Christmas Caroling season. Meanwhile, families drove through the neighbourhood to check out the lights, decorations, caroling and participate in the holiday fun.

Another big holiday we celebrated was Carnaval. My uncle owned a construction company and would provide a dump truck which we decorated and conditioned as a Float and joined the main Carnaval Parade.

My dad worked for Pan American Airways so most of the year we had people crashing on our sleeper sofa, (I never took notice of them except when I was on my way out to school). We also had a fairly large number of contacts around the world like an extended family which we would visit or they would visit us. So, I learned to be a gracious host at an early age.

Music was a large part of our lives. My dad would bring records from wherever in the world he would travel for work. Bossanova, Samba, American music of all sorts, Latin rhythms, Disco, Broadway Music, Jazz, all were played in my house.

I attended a boy's Catholic school with my brothers while my sisters attended a Girl's Catholic school. I started kindergarten at the Colegio San Agustín at the age of almost five years old and most of that year is a blur due to a bicycle accident where I sustained some head trauma. That would become a recurrent theme in my life as well as my nine lives (I should be on the eighth or so).

My nine lives are a joke about the many times when I could have or should have died but survived sometimes, completely unscathed but none the wiser. I remember that behind our school there was a very large esplanade for the school buses, (the school-owned their school buses), while the school buses were out taking kids home it was a very smooth area for bicycles riders, skaters and kids like me who would sit on the steps in front of the esplanade and wait to be picked up by our parents.

One day a kid asked me if I wanted to get a ride on his bike (I was four and a half years old so he was biking and I was riding on the back). We had picked up quite a bit of speed and he asked me if I wanted to go by the kiddie playground (where the Kindergarten was) and I told him that the gates were closed and that we would not be able to slip through with the bike. And as we approached the fence we got a little too close and one of the pedals got stuck on it. I assume that I flew off the bicycle and landed face down, since I don't remember anything but I was missing my four front teeth, thank God, they were the first set. I do remember sitting waiting for my mom and nothing else after that.

That is, until one day a little while later she was asked me if I wanted to repeat Kindergarten. Apparently, the priests at the Catholic school I attended were suggesting that I repeat Kindergarten as they were concerned about the injuries I had sustained during that accident. I recall telling her that I would not go back to that, and I was ready to leave the kiddie stuff behind and learn. My permanent teeth finally grew in when I was in the second grade, and I felt like a regular kid from then on.

Elementary school was a breeze, junior high and high school were nightmares that I could not wait to end. I hate to look back at it that way but hadn't it been for my family and the fun and love we had, I would not have made it.

I never had suicidal thoughts even through my hardest times in high school. But having witnessed some very effeminate guys being continuously taunted, made me aware that I should be careful who I spoke to about my sexual desires. Then again, I always knew once high school was over, I was free to start exploring where the men were, and also knew all along that it was nobody's business.

I was always optimistic that no matter how my day went, I'd pick up the next day and go back and face life again. That was my mom and dad's gift to me, not to give up and to have a hopeful attitude no matter what. They sought to protect me by giving me tools to survive not trying to change me.

My home was my shelter, my family and I were strong together and no matter how the world outside was, at home we had fun, love and laughs. I did not hang out with my school friends outside of school, unless there were special events like birthday parties. I had my neighbourhood friends and we all kept our school business out! LOL.

For three years, there was a local bully who tried to provoke me to fight, but he never got a reaction from me. Looking back, I sometimes wonder if should have gone for it, (I was taking Karate classes at the time). But, I knew that he and his buddies just wanted to kick my ass. He and I were in different classrooms for the last two years of high school and we never saw each other. From what I understand, he had a few bad breaks and was barred from graduation. From what I understand, he got his diploma later on in life. Interestingly enough, I saw him next at a reunion in 1991 where he hugged me and was very attentive through that whole evening. He still keeps in touch and is very cordial to me. By the way, every one of my classmates from Kindergarten to the twelfth grade knows that I am gay and most of them are cool with it. As for those who aren't, well who cares, I am happy.

The gay gene was making itself present in me at an early age. I remember having a crush on men at a very early age, (three years old). When I had reached age eleven, it kicked into high gear! I was like a heat-seeking missile out of control chasing my brothers' and sisters' male friends. I used intimate situations, like visiting some of them while they were alone, or while we were swimming together at a neighbour's pool to get close to them. Anyway, nothing sexual would ever happen besides catching a few of them naked while they showered or they changed clothes in front of me.

It was about this time that a neighbourhood boy about my age, showed me the ropes around self-pleasuring. We spent a lot of time together exploring, (nothing too invasive). Also around that time, I learned that other neighbourhood boys were exploring self-pleasuring with each other. I became curious, and played with one of them, but I felt more comfortable sticking with my buddy.

I was still in denial about my homosexuality until once at the age of sixteen, I found a college book from my oldest brother about human sexuality. It had graphic pictures of naked women and men, which gave me more of a thrill than any porn magazine that I have ever seen, even Playgirl! It had large pictures of circumcised men. I, being the only uncut member of my family, was rather shy about being naked in public, I was the kid who always explained why my cock was different from other boys, so I avoided being naked in front of others. For some reason the males in Panama, like the United States are mostly circumcised. The book gave me a glimpse of what naturally uncut men looked like.

Then in the word glossary there was a term that I had never heard before. It was Closet Queen, and was defined as a homosexual who does not accept his own homosexuality. That definition hit me hard! I knew then there was no running away from my homosexuality. Newly accepted sexual orientation and raging hormones make for a dangerous combination in a Catholic macho country, but at ten percent of the population plus any fence jumpers, (bisexuals), I stood a fair chance at meeting other gay men, as long as I was discreet. All my brothers and sisters had studied abroad, so I was pretty sure that I would also, so I would wait until I went to college to explore my newly accepted sexual orientation without too many inquisitive eyes…or so I thought.

I eventually attended Texas A&M in College Station, Texas, where I came out on March 22, 1983. A friend from Texas A&M who was openly gay, and with whom I had become good friends and his lover, took me out to Montrose, the Houston Gay district. I had never seen so many homosexual and gay-friendly people in one single place in my entire life! It was the confirmation that I needed that I was not alone, but I had no idea that there were so many of us! It was the greatest moment of my life apart from my first Gay Pride Celebration in Houston.

On February 24th, 1984 I met Paul, my first lover while cruising through Texas A&M Campus. We remained together for two and a half years, and remained close friends after we broke up. We had great times and had a large group of friends, but unfortunately, Paul was killed in a gay-bashing incident in Houston, on July 4th, 1991.

By that time, my parents wanted me to return to Panama. I was still hiding my homosexuality from them and many others down there. My parents gave me a warning to come home and stop wasting a lot of money or stay on my own. I decided to stay on my own.

The thing is, my temporary work visa had expired and I had basically no income. I was not authorized to work anymore, so I was essentially illegal in the US. I also made the mistake of dating a man who could be described as an opportunist. He dumped me after living rent-free at his apartment for the summer. He let me move in, then threw me out and kept my things. I basically became homeless.

But, by that time, a close friend offered me a job selling real estate with him in Houston. Plus, I had several friends that let me crash at their places, and I also had the job.

That was during 1988, the worst year of the AIDS times. There was no test for it, and no treatment yet. People were dying at such high rate that Texas gay publications were running free obituaries. It was a morbid show, but that was the first section we all looked at when opening those publications.

I started working on my residence, so I moved out of College Station to Houston in 1989. Through ups and downs, I got my US residence and was able to work and pay taxes. Met my second lover Johnnie and we moved to Montrose. Our home became the meeting place for all our friends. The location was unbeatable. Close enough to the clubs to walk and far enough to avoid the noise and drama.

I lived in that location for 19 years. It is now a large building in the West Gray Area of Houston. After that, I rented a house for two years. Shortly after my lease expired, a friend who I had known for years asked me to move in with her. Around that time, my job and I parted ways (and it benefitted me greatly because I had a large amount of unemployment insurance saved up), and moved with her because she needed a roommate. She had dated a couple of heterosexual friends and so, I trusted her. I had to give away, throw out and store anything that did not fit in her house. The space was limited so I did what I had to do. My new roommate and I joined a great (albeit expensive) gym.

We attended a Cardio Kickboxing class, and I must admit it was amazingly fun. If you want to feel high on Endorphins, that is the ticket.

During that time, I became a United States Citizen! Something of which I was really proud! But my roommate was going through a rough time. She had an Australian former lover whom she terrorized on a daily basis. She also saw a Psychologist once or twice a week. The Counselor took the brunt of my roommate´s verbal abuse. It seems that her readiness to fight and scream at people over small things got us banned from a restaurant which we loved, to the point that we were not even allowed deliveries. She also got into altercations with neighbours over small, silly things.

Built like she was, and her knowledge of self-defence, made her a formidable threat. All her drama got old really fast. I started seeking a way out. I told her that I could no longer live with her, especially after she had broken into her former lover's E-mail account.

A friend of mine in Fernandina Beach, Florida asked me to get away and come to see him. His name was Pete, an acquaintance whom I had met a few months before. He wanted me to look after his place while he was away for a while.

I decided that I had to leave my roommate's house and put most of my things in storage, packed my bags, loaded the car and left. I decided to spend the night at a friend's house and leave bright and early for Florida the next morning. The night before leaving for Florida turned out to be a story on its own!

My good friend Greg decided to throw a farewell orgy for me and somehow a happy male orgy turned into a potential Hitchcock movie. One attendee had a bad reaction to a drug called Spice, a synthetic form of marijuana. It has to be consumed in very small doses or it can have some scary effects! They eventually go away, depending on the amount consumed but the effects can range from 15 to 30 minutes in duration, which is what happened to this guy.

I was there to catch him before he hit the ground when he collapsed. I held him and made him comfortable as I reassured him that he would be fine (he could not talk or move except for his right hand which was shaking uncontrollably). Most of the attendees got dressed and left the house like they were leaving the scene of a crime. Only four of fifteen men were left: the host who was a nurse (hence why he was smoking Spice and not the real thing), a married man (with grown children) who was not out to his family, another friend of the host, and me, who was supposed to leave for Florida in the morning.

My friend, the nurse was trying to convince the young fellow that he had a low sugar episode, but he and everybody else knew it was the Spice. And so, the nurse started taking care of him, while he vomited on the nurse's naked body twice. The young man eventually fell asleep for thirty minutes and woke up as if nothing had happened!

I left for Florida on schedule the next morning.

Fernandina Beach is the northernmost city on Florida's Atlantic coast, on Amelia Island between Florida and Georgia. It is a marshy area with canals that connect the city to the Atlantic Ocean. It was a Slave trading spot and a Pirate hideout. Pete´s House was about one hundred yards from a Sixteenth-Century burial ground for Slaves. The slaves were mostly located in the back area of the cemetery.

In the house that Pete and I shared, our cell phones would not work properly and the internet was slow at best. I used to have to drive to a local marina to send and receive text messages, otherwise they would arrive a day or two late.

The night before I took Pete to the airport, there was a very strong and loud banging on the door, to the point that the door shook and vibrated a few inches open. Then there was another, so I grabbed the door and opened it forcibly. There was absolutely nothing or nobody there that could have hit or knocked on the door.

Pete yelled: "Now, you've let it in!!!" He was joking, of course, but I did not sleep well that night. There was, what seemed to be paranormal energy all over the place, especially at night. I went to sleep and kept my eyes closed regardless of what I heard or felt.

I spent a month there before going back to Houston with a clear idea of what I wanted to do. A great friend of mine who lived in Houston and a fellow Panamanian, suggested I go back to college. Which I did as soon as I got back to Houston.

So, when I returned, I started using my real name (Agustin) instead of my American Nickname: Auggie. I registered to study Horticulture at Houston Community College.

One night after class, while I relaxed in the apartment, I received a call from my former roommate's ex-lover, the

Australian, asking me if I had sent him a nasty e-mail. I told him that our only connection was my former roommate. Then I remembered borrowing her laptop once to check my e-mail. That was when I figured that she had broken into my e-mail and sent him a nasty one under my name.

I told him to seek police help. A month later as I was surfing the internet at home after class with the TV on in the other room, I heard the Australian´s name on the news and I quickly turned to see what he was up to. It turns out that my former roommate had been terrorizing him, vandalizing his home and even chased him with a medieval sword that he had gifted her. The news even showed her mugshot. She was the first female arrested in Houston for stalking. I had left that whole situation behind in the nick of time before things became newsworthy

I was attending college in my 50s, and while doing so I was able to travel to the former South Vietnam. We financed this trip through fundraising activities (plant sales) from our Horticulture club. We went during June and July 2012, and visited Saigon/Ho Chi Minh City, DaLat and Mui Né.

We were part of the Travel Abroad Program in college, and had a group of eleven students, an instructor, our Study Abroad counsellor, her brother, son and husband, who was a French photographer, and we rode a bus with two Vietnamese tour guides.

We visited many points of interest, including: The Museum of Remembrance, the Vietnamese homage to the

Cathedral Notre Dame, Markets, restaurants, we met Vietnamese farmers and helped them with planting and watering their crops. We were invited into their homes where we were humbled by joy and hospitality. They shared their food with us (bananas in this case). We visited several Buddhist temples. In DaLat we met the Lat, (the Indigenous people from the area).

Unlike the other students in our group, Paul, (a school buddy from HCC), and I participated in all activities, meeting natives and sharing food and drinks with them. In Mui Né we rented motorcycles and went riding with our guides. Paul and I would go to the beach in Mui Né and meet the fishermen at dawn with our guides to buy fresh seafood. We would learn about their lives and chat before our school group would wake up for breakfast.

In January 2013, I missed a week of classes because, as it turns out my blood sugar was at 600, something which I had no idea about. I had never had sugar problems before. I was told that I should have a stroke around 200! But here I am, almost ten years after, I am still diabetic and I am very healthy. I have it under control, although I slacked off working out with all this Covid thing, but I am getting back on that horse. If everything works out as my doctors want, they will take me off Insulin in a few months!

By the Summer of 2013, while visiting my family, I was told by my siblings that my parents were losing their cognitive capabilities rather fast and so, I finished my studies on a Friday December 21st, gave away most of my things, boxed up the rest (which a friend kept for me) and arrived in Panama on December 24th, 2013, that was my boomerang trajectory from, and back to Panama,

I am currently out and proud, living in Colombia, married to a Colombian man. My family knows, and the world does too (I was outed on Facebook by a suitor in 2010 or so, which is utterly ironic because he was afraid about his family and his former wife finding out, but she turned out to be a lesbian and his family had already pegged him as gay). My parents had never really accepted it before but after I went back, we worked it out. They met my husband and welcomed him into the family. My dad went to the grave in peace with me. My mom sometimes does not remember who he is, but she loves him. We are living in Colombia and are currently celebrating our 7th year together. We visit my mother and family 2 or 3 times a year. We are currently planning a trip to Panama for Christmas.

Acknowledgements

In 2018, Neil Fernyhough, the Program Coordinator of Alexandra House in Crescent Beach, BC, approached me to edit an anthology they were calling Sharing Our Journeys: Queer Elders Share Their Stories. It featured local Queer Elders who spoke openly about *coming out* back in the 1960s, 70s, and 80s when the world was a much different place. When it was published, this anthology proved to be popular with the general public.

With recent social movements like Black Lives Matter and Idle No More being at the forefront of positive social change, the timing is right for BIPOC and Trans Elders to step forward and share their stories with the world. This is a segment of the community that we very rarely hear from, and it's time to change that. The stories for this anthology are not only local but, indeed, international in scope. They tell us what it was like to grow up queer both inside and outside of North America.

I acknowledge all of the Queer BIPOC Elders who participated in this project: CJ Jackman-Zigante, Gloria Jackson-Nefertiti, Oscar Hall, Shinji Kasama, Cornell Thomas, Jayantha Withanage, and Agustin Restrepo. By opening up and sharing your stories, not only have you added so much to our collective queer history, you've shown the Queer Community more about your experiences as Queer BIPOC Elders.

To Neil Fernyhough, the Program Manager at Alexandra Neighbourhood House, for paving the way for both of the Sharing Our Journeys projects to become a reality.

To Rebecca Mabanglo-Mayor for all of your wonderful assistance and advice.

Zoe Duff and the fine people at Filidh Publishing who are very excited to be publishing both volumes of Sharing Our Journeys. And for generously donating a portion of all proceeds of this anthology to support the queer and multicultural programs at Alexandra Neighbourhood House.

Quirk-e: (Queer Imaging and Riting Kollective for Elders), an amazingly creative collective of Queer Elders in Vancouver, Canada whose members have supported this project right from the Get-Go!

And, of course, to my wonderful life partner, James Howard, for your ongoing support and love. I love you, babe.

Ron Kearse
Editor,
Sharing out Journeys 2:
Queer BIPOC Elders Tell Their Stories.

Ron Kearse

Ron was raised on military bases and has lived in most provinces in Canada. He's proud of his Celtic/Mohawk ancestry and honours both. He trained in broadcasting and volunteered his time to several community broadcasting projects, including Vancouver Cooperative Radio, Rogers Neighborhood Television (with the monthly show Gayblevision), and Radiogay.ca.

His writing credits include diverse genres such as: writing for businesses, novels and short stories, assistant writer for the television series Nations at War on the Aboriginal People's Television Network in Canada, local history, and blogs.

He worked with Aboriginal offenders for eight years and felt it was more of a calling than a job. He likes to travel and does so frequently because it inspires him.

(Photo credit: provided by author)

www.ingramcontent.com/pod-product-compliance
Lightning Source LLC
Chambersburg PA
CBHW070559180626
46817CB00005B/1909